JESUS IS BAE

JESUS IS BAE

A 31-Day Interactive Devotional
To Discover What It Means To Be In A
Relationship With Christ

Hanha Hobson & Jemeia Kollie

ELM HILL

A Division of
HarperCollins Christian Publishing

www.elmhillbooks.com

Jesus Is Bae
A 31-Day Interactive Devotional To Discover What It Means To Be In A Relationship With Christ

Published in Nashville, Tennessee, by Elm Hill, an imprint of Thomas Nelson. Elm Hill and Thomas Nelson are registered trademarks of HarperCollins Christian Publishing, Inc.

Elm Hill titles may be purchased in bulk for educational, business, fund-raising, or sales promotional use. For information, please e-mail SpecialMarkets@ ThomasNelson.com.

Scripture quotations marked ESV are from the ESV˚ Bible (The Holy Bible, English Standard Version˚). Copyright © 2001 by Crossway, a publishing ministry of Good News Publishers. Used by permission. All rights reserved.

Scripture quotations marked NASB are from New American Standard Bible˚. Copyright © 1960, 1962, 1963, 1968, 1971, 1972, 1973, 1975, 1977, 1995 by The Lockman Foundation. Used by permission. (www.Lockman.org)

Scripture quotations marked NIV are from the Holy Bible, New International Version˚, NIV˚. Copyright © 1973, 1978, 1984, 2011 by Biblica, Inc.˚ Used by permission of Zondervan. All rights reserved worldwide. www.Zondervan.com. The "NIV" and "New International Version" are trademarks registered in the United States Patent and Trademark Office by Biblica, Inc.˚

Scripture quotations marked NLT are from the Holy Bible, New Living Translation. © 1996, 2004, 2007, 2013, 2015 by Tyndale House Foundation. Used by permission of Tyndale House Publishers, Inc., Carol Stream, Illinois 60188. All rights reserved.

Library of Congress Cataloging-in-Publication Data

Library of Congress Control Number: 2018954515

ISBN 978-1-595559265 (Paperback)
ISBN 978-1-595559210 (eBook)

CONTENTS

Introduction

Thank you for joining me and Jemeia (*Jesus is Bae* series creator) as we all remind ourselves of our first love, Christ! We don't know about you, but we've struggled with spending quality time with Jesus, and we pray that this challenge changes all of that.

THE CHALLENGE:

For thirty-one days, we will commit to spending time with Jesus DAILY in whatever way that looks like. Maybe that's 30 minutes each day, or maybe it's 10 minutes. Perhaps it's listening to worship music or reading your Bible. Or a mix-up! Whatever it is, decide what is best for you and commit to it.

HOW IT WORKS:

When we think about relationships, many factors help them grow. What are some of your favorites? Time, communication, or conflict resolution might be a few. These are the same concepts we'll discuss and apply to our relationship with Jesus, and we'll reflect together on what it means to be in a relationship with Him—hence why Jesus is Bae (*before anyone else*).

To guide you in discovering Jesus as your bae, we have identified one ultimate goal, two areas of growth, and two challenges that will be broken up week by week. We have also provided you with reflection questions each day so that you can dig into the content and think about how it applies to you personally. These factors together will help you reflect on why we fell in love with this Man in the first place.

The goal is to **spend time with Jesus daily.** Achieving this goal is easier said than done, but it is so important. For you to relate to Jesus and know Him more intimately, you have to spend time with Him.

BRIEF OVERVIEW OF THE CONTENT:

Week 1: Prioritizing Time with Jesus
Week 2: Communicating with Jesus
Week 3: Addressing Habitual Sin and Discontentment
Week 4: Going on a Date with Jesus

We are incredibly thrilled to go on this journey with you, and it is our sincere prayer that upon completion of this challenge you will have started on a course to deepening intimacy and your relationship with Christ. After these short thirty-one days with Jesus Himself, you'll feel so full you may not want to stop (the actual goal). Your cup will run over, and you won't be spiritually thirsty anymore.

How do we know? Because that's the type of record Jesus has. In fact, He says it in His Word!

"I am the vine; you are the branches. If you remain in me and I in you, you will bear much fruit; apart from me you can do nothing."

— JOHN 15:5, NIV

We are believing in faith that this challenge will ignite a new passion inside of you. We hope it's a small journey of self-discovery, and we pray that as you dive deeper into the Word, you'll experience God in a new way. We pray that you will uncover and understand who He is in your life.

Hanha Hobson
Founder of Transparency Blog

PRIORITIZING TIME WITH JESUS

PRIORITIZING TIME WITH JESUS

This week, we are focusing on our first area of growth—prioritizing time with Jesus. This area of growth goes hand-in-hand with our ultimate goal of spending time with Jesus daily.

It is not possible to spend time with Jesus daily if you don't prioritize your time with Him. God has a lot to say and He cherishes the time He can spend with you, but you have to be willing to give Him your undivided time and attention.

Take a look at your relationships. How can you get to know someone if you barely talk to them or spend time with them? I'm pretty sure if a woman or man treated you like this, you wouldn't consider yourself in a relationship with them.

Think about it. If spending time with your significant other is essential to growing in your relationship, then it is 100 times more important with the God of the universe, your Father, your first love, Jesus.

Here are two quotes from Francis Chan that are convicting.

"When we love God, we naturally run to Him—frequently and zealously. Jesus didn't command that we have a regular time with Him each day. Rather, He tells us to 'love the Lord your God with all your heart and with all your soul and with all your mind.' He called this the 'first and greatest commandment' (Matt. 22:37–38, NIV). The results are intimate prayer and study of His Word. Our motivation changes from guilt to love."

Okay, listen. This quote is CRAZY. The gist is that you make time for what is important to you and for the ones you love and want to be intentional with.

The key word is *love*. And love is a matter of the heart. Without love, spending time with Jesus will be another item on your checklist.

"There is no substitute for being alone with God. If you don't have time, you need to quit something to make room. Skip a meal. Cancel a meeting. End some regular commitment. There is literally nothing more important you could do today. God literally determines whether or not you take another breath. "He himself gives to all mankind life and breath and everything". (<u>Acts 17:25, ESV</u>)

Could anything be more important than meeting with the One who decides if you live through this day? Could anything be better? How can we not make time to be with the Maker of time? What plans do you have today that you think so important that you would race past the Creator to get to them?"

PHEW! This one speaks for itself!
We encourage you to do the following this week:

1. Identify a time and place during your day where you KNOW that you can give God your best and undivided attention.
2. Commit to that time and place for the rest of this week. Observe and record the benefits of this.

WEEK 1 RESOURCES

1. The Greatest Thing You Could Do Today (A blog post on spending time with God)
2. How to Study the Bible (a blog post)
3. 10 Ways to Remove Distractions & Choose God First (a blog post)
4. Women of the Word: How to Study the Bible with Both Our Hearts and Our Minds by Jen Wilkin
5. Going Deeper: Bible Study Resources (a blog post)

DAY 1 - JOHN 14:5–14

Say you live in a dying world and you are one of the few people who knows about the cure that can help everyone live. I forgot to mention that you're also the hero in this storyline and, like every good story, you know that there's no way you'll be able to help all the sick people without a fight. You know your enemy is going to do everything in his power to prevent you from obtaining that cure, and then do everything in his power to stop you from sharing it with other people.

When we think about it, our walks with Jesus work in the same way. Jesus is the cure. In John 14:6 NIV, it says that He is the way, the truth, and the life and no one can get to the Father except through Him. The truth is we do live in a dying world, and the fact is you do have the cure. Jesus.

But you must understand the enemy's strategy. He is going to use every distraction in his book to stop you from spending time with God: I'm too tired to wake up earlier in the morning, life is so busy, I don't know what to do during my time with Him, I'm too tired to do it before I go to bed, or my personal favorite, I just don't feel like it. Some are excuses, but all of them are distractions.

And why would the enemy distract you from spending time with your Creator? Because the more you spend time with God, the more you become who He has made you to be. The more you understand your calling, the more you can help others find Him, and the more you begin to experience freedom because of the redeeming work on the cross.

The problem is not whether Jesus works. You will always feel refreshed after spending time with Him! He says it in His Word. Draw near to God, and He will draw near to you (James 4:8, ESV), or He will fill you with joy in His presence (Psalm 16:11, NIV). The problem is making God a priority and taking a moment to carve out time to actually do it. It's difficult. We completely understand how that feels, but so much value comes from it.

You have to protect your time with God, and you will have to fight for your relationship with Him. Decide now that you'll take some time to discover what works best for your schedule this week. And then decide that you will sit and pray for 10–15 minutes no matter who or what tries to stop you.

Action Item/Reflection:

1. Identify the time and place where you KNOW that you can give God your undivided attention. Is it in the morning, evening, before you go to bed, in between class, while your baby is napping? List those out and commit to it this week.

2. What stood out to you, personally, in John 14:5–14?

DAY 2 - MARK 1:35–37

For many Christians, mornings are both the ideal and hardest times to spend time with the Lord. In a day and age where so many people and commitments are stealing our time and energy, it is only human to want to get every bit of sleep we can.

Being a student, a professional in healthcare, law, business, and even in a variety of service jobs requires us to care for the needs of people daily. Life tests our minds and bodies, and it is natural for us to want to recharge adequately, particularly in the morning.

Believe it or not, Jesus was just like us. He was fully God, but He was also fully human. Jesus had just as many, maybe even more, commitments than we do and none of it was ideally scheduled. All day He was pouring Himself out to people, so they were healed and saved. Think about the woman with the issue of blood. By her merely touching His garment, Jesus released His power, and she was healed.

Jesus' days were never about Him. He came to save the world and each day of His ministry reflected that. If that wasn't enough, this man had NO breaks. He even died nailed to a cross! To fulfill God's will, Jesus knew He had to prioritize time with the Father first thing in the morning.

Why? Because all was still and quiet. He knew that the morning, while it was still dark, was the prime time for Him to commune with the Lord without distractions or commitments. For Him, it recharged and empowered Him to conquer the day ahead.

Without spending time with God, there was no way He could show the world the saving power of the Gospel. How many of us think that way? That there is NO way we can be the best student, professional, spouse, or parent without spending time with God? Or do we think we can do it all on our own?

Maybe mornings are not an ideal time for you. Perhaps you work super early, are in school and continuously exhausted, or have a newborn baby or kids that you need to tend to in the morning. That's completely understandable.

We just challenge you to identify a time and place where you can commune with God in stillness and quiet. For Jesus, that was in the morning. But maybe it's 10 p.m. after homework or tucking in the kids. Whatever it is, find that time where you can give God your best and feel recharged.

Action Item/Reflection:

1. What is hindering you from having a consistent time with the Lord? List any obstacles out and strategize a plan to help you overcome those barriers so that you can start having more consistent time with God.

DAY 3 - MATTHEW 22:37

Loving God first and foremost, and then loving people as you love yourself is God's greatest commandment. Matthew 22:37, NIV, says that the way to love God is to love Him with <u>ALL</u> our heart, soul, and mind. The tricky part is that love is not merely a feeling; love is an act. More specifically, the Bible tells us that to love God is to obey Him. In John 14:15, NIV, Jesus says "If you love me, keep my commands."

So how do we do that? Let's break it down.

Loving God with All of Our Heart

The Bible tells us that we should guard our hearts because everything flows from it (Proverbs 4:23). To love God with our heart, we must surrender our desires and motivations to Him.

No, we don't hide the things in our hearts from Him because He is all-knowing. Instead, we are honest with Him about who we are, what we feel, and what we want. Then we assess what is in our heart, compare them to His standards, and surrender any motive or desire that is not pleasing to Him or does not align with His will.

WE. HOLD. NOTHING. BACK. We give our desires to God and ask Him to create in us a new and clean heart (Psalm 51:10). His command, not suggestion, is to love Him with our hearts. That means His will, not ours.

Loving God with All of Our Mind

Romans 12:2 warns us not to conform to the patterns of this world, but to be transformed by the renewing of our mind. Philippians 4:8

charges us to think of what is true, noble, right, pure, lovely and admirable. Living out these verses is what it means to love God with our mind. This is not something we can do passively. It takes an effort to hold captive thoughts that don't represent God and make them obedient to Christ (2 Corinthians 10:5).

Loving God with All of Our Soul

To love God with our soul is to love Him with our whole life. It encompasses a combination of both loving Him with our mind and heart. We give Him our everything—thoughts, feeling, perceptions, desires, beliefs, career, families, relationships, job, studies, etc.

We surrender everything to God and pursue Him through the lens of His love. It's not enough to love Him when it's easy or when things seem to fall into place. The real test lies in our ability to love Him when it costs us.

Jesus' life on earth and death displayed this truth. Additionally, He articulated this perfectly in John 15:13, NIV, when He said to His disciples, "Greater love has no one than this: to lay down one's life for one's friends." It cost Jesus everything to die for us, but He did it anyway.

So how does loving God tie into this week's theme of prioritizing time with Jesus? In a society where we are always on the go with SO many people and things taking up our time, it's easy to forget Jesus. Perhaps because we can't physically see Him and there is no strict time required to meet with Him.

But if our hearts truly desire Him, if He is always on our minds, and if our souls thirst for Him, love will compel us to go no days without being with our maker, friend, and lover. You might read this and think "I am not capable of this kind of love." Let us encourage you that it is impossible to love (obey) God the way He deserves.

But He is a just and compassionate God who sees our hearts and desires to give Him our all. With the help of the Holy Spirit, you are capable of loving Him and giving Him your best just as you would your spouse, children, friends, parents, etc. Don't strive to prioritize time with Jesus on your own. Rely on His help.

Action Item/Reflection:

1. In your own words, what does the quality and quantity of your time with God say about your love for Him?

2. What does it look like for you to love God with your heart, mind, and soul?

DAY 4 - JOHN 15

The thing about living in today's society is that we live in a self-sufficient culture. The "I can do it all by myself" mentality is something that is crippling our generation when it comes to our spiritual development.

We cannot do anything without God (John 15:5). We must remain in Him by spending consistent time with Him. The Greek word used in this context is the word *menõ*, which means *to dwell, endure, or remain as one and not become different*. Jesus repeats this concept over and over in the chapter, so it must be a critical point!

Failure to recognize our need for the Savior is why we experience problems like pride or discontentment. The Bible has many scriptures about being humble, and living in a state of humility is recognizing that you will always have a need or a gap.

God did that so that you would be dependent on Him to provide. It's why scripture says, "The Lord is my Shepherd, I lack nothing" (Psalm 23:1, NIV). It's why you're strong when you are weak because God's grace is sufficient (2 Corinthians 12:9–10). We lack nothing because God fills those gaps and makes us whole.

When we are prideful, we try to fill the gaps ourselves. We think we can do it on our own, but God is the only one who has the infinite power to live in that role. True fulfillment only comes from Him as it says in verse 11.

Recognize your need for Jesus today, but know that there is no pressure when it comes to God's love! The goal is to not remain in your love for Him, but instead to remain in HIS love for you!

Action Items/Reflection:

1. What are some needs you should surrender to God so that He can take control and fill your gaps?

2. How can you remind yourself to remain in God's love, especially when it comes to your lack?

15

DAY 5 - PSALM 91

Protection is a theme in Psalm 91. In the very last part of the chapter, we see that God honors those who love Him and those who acknowledge Him by protecting or rescuing them from evil or their enemies. Additionally, He hears and responds to those who call on His name.

The Lord promises that if we abide and remain in Him and make Him our refuge, He will command the angels to guide and protect us in all of our ways. We do not have to fear in His presence, especially when we are walking in His will. These are examples of His steadfast promises to us. Isn't that awesome?

How often do we go days without even acknowledging Him? Or how often do we rush out of His presence because we have reached the time limit we set to spend with Him? How many of us know that the battle is not against flesh and blood, but against principalities and evil forces (Ephesians 6:12)?

We are only fooling ourselves if we think that life is entirely about what we see in the natural. There is a whole spiritual realm, an enemy who only comes to steal, kill, and destroy (John 10:10). In fact, just as God commands His angels concerning us, the enemy has an agenda for us, and He uses His demons to do it.

It is so important that we do not take the power of God's protection lightly. Each time we go a day without acknowledging God we are ignoring our Creator, the only being who knows our beginning to end, who holds our lives in the palm of His hand and is always one step ahead of our enemies and Satan.

He is the only one who knows what is working against us and can intervene on our behalf. He doesn't need our time or help. He can take care of us by Himself. But He certainly would like to keep us in the loop, and it's not a bad idea to take time to praise and thank Him for His protection.

Spending time with God daily and acknowledging Him, even if He seems distant, is understandably hard. But His word is true. He promises never to leave us or forsake us. He is not a man that He should lie. So, if He promises that He will protect those who love Him enough to dwell in Him, then we can rest assured that He will stay true to that promise too.

Action Item/Reflection:

1. Are you in a place right now where you are desperately in need of God's protection? Do you truly believe in your heart that the Lord is your refuge and that you can safely dwell in Him? Why or why not?

2. How do you feel that time with God will help you access more of Him and His power?

DAY 6 - MATTHEW 14:13–15

Let's dive right into the text today! Jesus has just heard that his best friend and cousin, John the Baptist, has been murdered, and now King Herod is out to get Him too. Jesus then tries to get a moment to Himself and focus on getting to safety while a ton of people is following Him, asking Him to fix their problems.

We don't know about you, but if that were us in that position, we would probably lose it. Place yourself in Jesus's shoes. Someone you love and deeply care about has just been killed, you have to get yourself out of harm's way, and now there are people you don't even know asking you for help.

Jesus knew how to set the bar high! Because instead of getting angry or annoyed, He has compassion on the people. He heals them AND then provides for them by performing one of His greatest miracles. He feeds 5,000 men with only two fish and five loaves of bread. Mind you. We're not even counting the wives and children.

But if Jesus did it for them, He will most certainly do it for you! He doesn't necessarily *need* us, but He does want a relationship with us. John 15:16 says that we didn't choose Him, He chose us. You are not an inconvenience to God.

When you received salvation, Jesus invited you into an intimate relationship with Him, and He's in this for the long haul, for eternity. Literally! He loves it when you come talk to Him and spend quality time in His presence. God is always present, but worship and time with Him draw Him close.

Again we see another example through the context of scripture where people have recognized their need for Jesus. They made Him a priority, and I'm not sure if they had any other choice. Some people may have been dying. Some probably thought that Jesus was their only hope. Whatever their issue was, they went to find the Healer. Some even traveled great lengths to follow Jesus even when He had to leave town.

Will you position your heart in the same way? Will you have this same posture of desperation even when you have a significant to-do list? Will you love God with your whole heart, soul, mind, and strength? It's no secret that a real relationship takes time, discipline, and effort. But God's burden is easy, and His yoke is light (Matthew 11:30).

Action Item/Reflection:

1. What are some things you can do to grow in your relationship with God?

DAY 7 - PSALM 1

Think about the closest people in your life—maybe it's your parents, your children, your best friends, or your significant other. When it comes to those relationships, you probably love to spend time with them. You usually go out of your way or do whatever you can to make them happy. Because you love and care about them, you have a natural sense of selflessness. You're willing to give them your time and effort.

We should see our relationship with God in the same way! It shouldn't feel tiring. If you felt like you HAD TO spend time with someone, you would think they were burdensome or draining. But many of us sometimes feel that way towards God. Our time with Him feels like a chore rather than a desire.

Let's be honest. There will be moments when you may not feel like getting up and spending time with God, but we should change our perspective and understand that each moment with Him is not an obligation but an opportunity. We get to have an encounter with Christ. We get to enter into His presence. We get to magnify His name!

Truly desiring God will lead to the decision of making Him a priority. Like your natural relationships, you will do whatever you can to make Him happy, not because you have to prove anything to Him, but because you love Him! Don't wait until you feel like it. Instead, have faith. Faith says you could if you would! Lead with faith first, then the desire will follow.

When we prioritize God, we begin to live in His ways. We get to know Him better, and we discern His desires. Like Psalm 1:2 says, spend time with God consistently. Spend time with Him in the morning and at night. Spend time with Him when things are going good and when things are going bad. Spend time with Him when you have clarity and understanding, and when you are confused and unsure of what's going on.

If you're struggling with making God a priority, ask Him to change the desires of your heart. This is a prayer I GUARANTEE He will answer! Pray that He would reveal His love for you and allow you to see yourself the way that He sees you.

Action Item/Reflection:

1. Write down a prayer and ask God to align your desires with His. Pray that you would grow more in love with Him.

WEEK 1 REFLECTION

How did week 1 go? Reflect on this past week and record what you learned about making God a priority. Did you spend time with God daily? Write down any changes or benefits you noticed. If you missed a day, write down your observations about that too.

COMMUNICATING WITH JESUS

COMMUNICATING WITH JESUS

This week, we are focusing on our second area of growth—communicating with Jesus. Like a necklace, we hope that you can see how the pieces of this challenge are coming together. Spending time with Jesus is connected to prioritizing time with Him, and as you spend more time with Him, you are better able to communicate with Him.

In any romantic relationship, communication is key. For you to understand and grow in a relationship with your significant other, not only do you have to be intentional about communicating with them, but you also have to listen to what they have to say.

The same applies to an intimate relationship with Jesus. Jesus knows you better than anyone. He knows when you sit and when you rise. He perceives your thoughts from afar. He's familiar with all your ways. And before a word on your tongue is spoken, He knows it completely! (Psalm 139:1–4)

How much more important is it that you are intentional with communicating and listening to Him?

We love this quote by Tim Keller:

"Like a baby learning language, we learn how to communicate with God by listening to His words first."

And this one too.

"To be loved but not known is comforting but superficial. To be known and not loved is our greatest fear. But to be fully known and truly loved is, well, a lot like being loved by God. It is what we need more than anything. It liberates us from pretense, humbles us out of our self-righteousness, and fortifies us for any difficulty life can throw at us."

You have direct access to this love—to be known AND loved. We want you to experience all of it to its fullest potential!

This week, we encourage you to do two things:

1. BE INTENTIONAL ABOUT PRAYER AND COMMUNICATING WITH JESUS.

This is YOUR communication with Him. This could be through prayer, journaling, or just talking to Him vocally. Think about how you communicate in your relationships with people. Try to do the same in your relationship with Christ.

2. BE WILLING TO LISTEN.

This is HIS communication with you. God has a lot to say about you, your day, life, future, and also about Him and His Character. However, it's not enough to just give God your burdens and exit from His presence. It's not okay to only come to Him when you are in need of Him.

I mean He'll still love you, but don't you want more? Can you give Him more of your heart? Can you make HIM the center of it all instead of your prayer time being all about you and what you want?

We urge you, in addition to communicating your thoughts and heart to Him, to take time to listen to what He has to say back.

He may speak to your heart, speak through a person, give you a conviction, or point you to scripture. There is NO limit to How God communicates. Just trust that He will show you more of Himself in a unique way that only you will understand.

This may be challenging, but it will produce amazing long-term benefits.

WEEK 2 RESOURCES

1. Anxieties: To be Cast Not Carried (a sermon)
2. How to Pray (a sermon and a personal favorite)
3. God Hears and Responds (a sermon)
4. God Listens and Responds (a sermon)
5. How does one pray? ACTS Model (a blog post)
6. Does the Holy Spirit Live in You? (a blog post)
7. When God is Silent (a podcast)
8. How to Hear from God Sermon Series (a sermon series)
9. Prayer: Experiencing Awe and Intimacy with God by Tim Keller
10. Becoming a Prayer Warrior by Elizabeth Alves

PRAYER PROMPTS

ADORATION

1. Tell God how awesome He is
2. Tell God how sovereign He is
3. Tell God how beautiful His creation is (including you)
4. Tell God that you love Him
5. Tell God that He is amazing
6. Tell God that He is glorious
7. Tell God you honor Him
8. Tell God He is faithful
9. Tell Him that He is perfect

CONFESSION

1. Sins you need to confess
2. Areas of your life that are not pleasing to God
3. Mistreating those around you
4. Hurts you are still holding onto
5. Burdens that overwhelm you
6. People you are struggling to forgive
7. Thinking wrongly about yourself
8. Someone who grieves you

THANKSGIVING

1. Thank God for His love
2. Thank God for Jesus and your salvation
3. Thank God for the Holy Spirit and His guidance
4. Thank God for His grace and mercy
5. Thank God for His favor
6. Thank God for your health
7. Thank God for providing (house, clothes, etc.)
8. Thank God for His presence

SUPPLICATION

1. Nation and World (missionaries, president)
2. Community (your church, children's school, your job, etc.)
3. Family and friends (their needs)
4. Career and dreams you have
5. Courage to step out on faith
6. Fruit of the spirit you are lacking
7. For God to perform a miracle
8. For understanding and wisdom
9. For God to reveal your talents and gifts
10. Peace regarding insecurities
11. Prayer to overcome doubt

DAY 8 - LUKE 3:21–23

There are many ways that the Lord can speak and communicate with us. However, one sure way to hear from Him is through His word. Furthermore, prayer is how we can speak to Him directly. How many of us feel like that is not enough at times?

How many of us reach times in our lives when God seems so distant when it is hard to conceptualize being vulnerable to a God that you cannot see or even audibly hear? How many of us have caught ourselves running to leaders, friends, and our significant others, instead of God, for advice or answers that only God can give us?

We know that feeling all too well, but we hope that today's verse will encourage you to run to God first. In this week's verse, we see that when John baptized Jesus, and ONLY when Jesus prayed:

1. The heavens opened up, and the Holy Spirit appeared in the form of a dove.
2. The Father responded and spoke to Jesus personally saying, "You are my son and I am pleased with you."

The Father's response at that moment was so personal to Jesus. It was displayed by the Holy Spirit ascending from Heaven, and not in the form of a shapeless ghost. Now, let's be real. Most of us imagine the Holy Spirit to be a ghost, or maybe we just have no concept of what the Holy Spirit even looks like. That's beside the point, but the Holy Spirit came down like a dove, like a creature that we humans can easily see and conceptualize. The way that the Holy Spirit met Jesus was very personable.

Additionally, the Father Himself spoke to Jesus personally,

affirming Jesus's identity and the fact that He was so pleased with His Son. This is amazing! But often it's easy to downplay just how profound this verse is because our expectations are so low when we come to God and read the Bible.

We either feel like the Bible is too broad, doesn't apply to us today, or we just can't grasp what Jesus went through so that we can be adopted as sons and daughters of God. If you truly understand that you are not an orphan anymore, a verse like this and Jesus's experience while being baptized would not seem so farfetched.

This verse is so encouraging because it shows that when we read the Bible and pray, God will respond in a way that is unique to us. That is the beauty of today's verse. God speaks in ways that are unique to us because He knows each of us individually and intimately. We just need to pray that He will help our hearts be continuously reminded of His love, help us trust that He is faithful to meet with us when we commit to communicating and spending time with Him.

So today, we challenge you to make use of the two most powerful tools in communicating with God—the Bible and prayer. Trust that He is always near. You don't have to strive to earn anything from him. Just trust and be, friend.

Action Item/Reflections:

1. What was one thing that stood out to you from this verse about how God communicates to us?

2. What did He speak to you personally?

DAY 9 - 1 CORINTHIANS 2

When you received salvation, you admitted your sin; you believed Jesus is the son of God who died on the cross to forgive you of that sin, and you confessed your faith in Him. Do you know what that means? It means as soon as you prayed that prayer, the Holy Spirit came and took residence inside your heart (1 Corinthians 3:16).

It's easy to overcomplicate seeking the Lord and His wisdom, but the Holy Spirit is our secret weapon. He is one of the three persons who make up the Trinity, and He has the very same essence and characteristics of God. 1 Corinthians 2:11, NIV, says, "No one knows the thoughts of God except the Spirit of God."

Let that sink in a bit. This Spirit of God also known as the Holy Spirit lives inside you. YOU! This is why we're able to confidently say that we have the mind of Christ, because the Holy Spirit serves as our guide. When it comes to communicating with God, we have to believe that God has something to reveal to us. We have to believe the scripture when it says that we'll be able to understand the plans God has for us, because the Holy Spirit will reveal it (1 Corinthians 2:9–10).

Hebrews 4:12–13 says that the Word of God is alive and active. It is sharper than any double-edged sword, and it penetrates deep into the dividing soul and the spirit. It judges the thoughts and attitudes of the heart.

God wants you to understand Him better. When He died on the cross, it's so He could have a relationship with you. He wouldn't have gone through all of that suffering, rejection, and pain not to share anything. He wouldn't go through all of that so that you know nothing about Him!

The next time you dive into your Word, ask God to communicate with you. Ask Him to reveal more of Himself to you. And believe that He will! James 1:5–7 says that God loves to give His wisdom generously. He says that if you ask Him for it, He will give it to you. But there's a catch! You must believe. Otherwise, you shouldn't expect to receive anything.

Ask and believe! He won't fail you.

Action Item/Reflection:

1. What do you think are some thoughts you say to yourself that intimidate you from reading your Bible or praying to God? Write them here.

2. Now write down a prayer and ask God to free you from those thoughts. Find a scripture that counteracts these thoughts and write them here.

DAY 10 - MATTHEW 6:5–15

This passage of scripture is what we call the model prayer. It's an example of Jesus Himself praying, and it is especially helpful for those who don't know how to pray. No matter where you are in your prayer life—whether you're a beginner and don't know what to do, or if you've been praying every day for the last ten years—there is nothing like getting back to the basics and examining the way we communicate with God.

There is power in prayer. It is a place where you can not only communicate with God but also receive His counseling and advice. It's a place where you can cast your cares on Him (1 Peter 5:7) and learn more about yourself and the areas of your life that need growth. Although the ACTS Model isn't the same exact way Jesus prayed, it is relatively similar and a simple and easy guide to follow. The acronym stands for adoration, confession, thanksgiving, and supplication.

As we see in Matthew, Jesus begins praying by first acknowledging God, and uses the intimate word *Father* to reflect the personal relationship He has with Him. He then acknowledges the fact that God's name, will, and kingdom takes priority above anything else. These verses can fall under the category of adoration. It's Jesus's form of worship, and we should begin our prayers this way as well. When we pray, we should first enter into God's presence with praise and thanksgiving (Psalm 100:4).

Next, Jesus asks God to provide for His needs. This included daily provision, forgiveness, and strength. These verses can fall under the category of confession and supplication. Provision for the day since tomorrow has enough worries of its own (Matthew 6:34), forgiveness for sins, and strength to overcome temptation and fight this fight of faith. When you pray, confess your sins and ask God to supply all of your needs, whatever those needs are.

Jesus ends His prayer in thanksgiving, and that's our cue that we should too. Begin and end your prayer with praise. Thank God for what He has done, what He is doing, and what He will do in your life.

Can we end today's devotional in prayer?

Father, you are so holy and perfect. You are majestic and worthy of every single praise that we can give you. There is no one like you, God. No one greater, no one higher, no one better. Thank you for sending your son Jesus to die on the cross for our sins so that we can spend eternity with you. Thank you for the time that we get to spend with you today.

Forgive us of our sins. Cleanse us of anything that is not like you. Take our broken and contrite spirits and restore to us the joy of our salvation. Forgive us for the things that we don't even know anything about.

But thank you for the woman reading this devotional. Thank you for her willingness to get to know you better. Thank you that she is taking time to discover what it means to be in a relationship with you. Be with her today and every day. Help her to know that you are sovereign and in control. Help her to realize that you have created her with intention and that you've called her for a purpose. Give her the peace that surpasses all understanding, and help her to seek you with all her heart, soul, mind, and strength.

Thank you for her life, Father. Bless her in a new way. Open her eyes so that she can see herself the way that you see her. You are so worthy and we love you. We pray all these things in your precious and holy name, Amen.

Action Item/Reflection:

1. Take some time to learn how you can follow this model of prayer in Matthew. Then take some time to review the prayer prompts provided in week 2 resources. Either write down your prayer in a journal or pray out loud.

DAY 11 - JOHN 10

John 10 reaffirms two truths for believers:

1. Jesus is a good Shepherd who laid down His own life for us.
2. We are His sheep, and we know His voice.

The most significant thing that Jesus did for us was lay down His life for us. He was abandoned by the Father and nailed to the cross so that we would never feel alone in any circumstance that we face. That, my friends, is the Gospel. Because Jesus conquered the cross, everything else is a lesser thing. Because He gave us the gift of salvation, any other mountain or valley that we have to overcome is small. This is who He says He is—our Redeemer, our Friend, our Shepherd, our First Love.

To be His sheep means to wholeheartedly trust first and foremost in who God says He is—our good shepherd who will never lead us astray or into danger. To be His sheep is to trust in His steadfast love, the love that compelled Him to go to the cross for us and the love that is dedicated to purifying us until we see Him in eternity. It means to believe deep in your heart that you can discern His voice and direction.

Now, let us caution you. To experience what it means to be God's sheep, you must get to know Him, and that comes through spending time with Him, being in the Word and being faithful to communicate with Him through prayer.

What happens when you do all of those things and still feel like you cannot hear Him or you hear His voice wrong? Let us help you. Imagine that you are a baby learning to walk for the first time. Picture the moment when you start to take your first steps. All is well until you head down the stairs, which is obviously dangerous because you are a baby and upon stepping on the stairs, you could fall!

Now, imagine that just before you take that first step, your father quickly runs to you, redirects you, and then puts a boundary right in front of the stairs so that you don't walk into danger again. Friends, this is what Jesus, our good Shepherd, does for us.

As His sheep, sometimes we don't know when we are headed down the wrong track, relationship, or situation, etc. We just don't know! But the beauty of being His sheep is that Jesus has us covered. We never have to fear because He is faithful. Even when you are unsure as to whether or not you heard God, know that He directs the moments that feel like dead ends. The journey is never wasted.

Action Item/Reflection:

1. Reflect on a time when you felt like you heard from God, headed down a path, but realized you reached a dead end. Maybe it was the wrong job, rejection, or a relationship. It can be anything. Where do you feel God was in that moment? What are some ways that you think He was directing you?

2. What are truths that you are choosing to remember today? That remind you of your identity as His sheep?

DAY 12 - PSALM 116

In Psalm 116, you can just sense the passion and emotion from the scripture. There's no limit to what David shares with God, and he lays it all out at His feet. The way that David pours out His heart to God is the same way that you can too. And why's that? Let's discuss.

God is always available.

He's available in every sense of the word—emotionally, spiritually, and mentally. Even in the moments when you don't want to show up for him, God is still available for you. It doesn't matter if it's eleven o'clock at night, God still wants to hear from you. He wants you to cast your burdens from the day on Him, and He wants to forgive you of your sins as you repent.

That's the beauty of Jesus. He cares so deeply for you that He will always be available. When NO ONE seems to answer the phone or when you're feeling super lonely or misunderstood, God is still there to talk, and He never fails to understand you. Just like Jeremiah 33:3 says, you can call to Him and He will tell you great and unsearchable things you do not know.

He knows you by name.

That seems so simple, but it is so powerful. When we take the time to think about who God is, this Man created the entire universe. EVERYTHING. The birds, the trees, the water, and the millions of people who are currently living on the planet not to mention the people who have already died. That is A LOT of people, and He knows you personally.

Intimately. Deeply. By name. He can spot you in a crowd of thousands, and He knows the smallest details about you. In fact, He takes pride in it. You don't go unnoticed by Him. Louie Giglio puts it best,

"God knows you better than you know yourself. He knows just how small and frail you are. He knows you're just one person, a tiny one at that. He knows your limitations, and He made you that way for a purpose. That's why God never asks you to be more than you are—and why He always stands ready to be your constant supply. God knows that you are weak, and He is in touch with just how potent He Himself is."

He is the Great I Am.

When you just take time to get to know Jesus (which is what you're doing by reading this book), you can't help but scream how worthy He is. It's not even about what He's done or what He's capable of doing. You just want to go crazy because He is who He is. He is perfect, holy, and majestic. He is creative, beautiful, and sovereign. He cares for you when no one else does, and the best part is that He's faithful. He is the Great I Am.

God isn't going anywhere. He specifically gave us Jesus so that we could spend eternity with Him. This is what a personal relationship with Him looks like. You won't be able to find a better best friend. You can tell Him all your secrets. You can share it all too, just as David did because the grace and love you experience on a daily basis are more than we deserve for a lifetime.

Action Item/Reflection:

1. Think about a best friend in your life. Now think about your relationship with Jesus. Do you think you trust God and pour your heart out to Him as you would a best friend? Try doing that in the space below.

2. Challenge yourself just to worship God today. For a moment, don't ask for anything. Just list out His characteristics and thank Him for who He is. Write the ABC's of adoration below—list an adjective to describe God with each letter of the alphabet.

DAY 13 - JOHN 1:1–18

Behold, THE WORD, better known as GOD, took on humility as JESUS. Can we just let that sink in? Why would He do that? I mean He is GOD, He is holy, He is majestic. We can't touch Him, and we can't get to His level. Angels have to cover up just to be in His presence, and He left His spotless throne to come to crusty old earth (LOL, kidding).

On a serious note, He did all of that; yet when He lived among us, we didn't even receive Him well. In fact, we rejected Him. The climax of the greatest story ever told, the Gospel, took place when Jesus humbled Himself to the point of death, died nailed to a cross, then rose within three days in triumphant glory.

Does that give you chills? He did that for YOU. He did that because He wanted to adopt you as a son or daughter of God. You were dead in your sin. But instead of giving you what you deserve, which is eternal damnation, He laid down His life out of compassion and love for you. Now you are His child, and you have full access to the throne room. Can you imagine? Each day that you awake His arms are wide open, and He is eager to meet with you, embrace you, and shower you with His love.

That means that you can openly communicate with Him. He knows all things, and you do not have to guard your heart or hold back when you are in His presence. He is the only one who knows you so intimately and can speak into your life in ways that only you can understand.

Do not downplay the amazing access you have to the God of the universe, the One who was there in the beginning and the One who is eager to walk with you till the end. You are His child. Embrace and boldly approach His throne. Humble yourself and pour your heart out to Him. He is near today.

Action Item/Reflection:

1. Identify some areas of your heart that you have guarded against God. Reflect on why you felt like you needed to hide those areas from Him.

2. What truth are you speaking towards that area today? We challenge you to uncover those things before God.

DAY 14 - DANIEL 6

Daniel in the lions' den is a classic Bible story. Daniel is currently working as a government administrator, and he is doing so well for himself that the king is considering him for a promotion. Daniel was brilliant in what he did, and as you can guess, some of the other government leaders were not happy about it. No matter how hard they tried they couldn't find anything wrong with Daniel, so they did the only thing they could do: they decided to use His relationship with God against him.

This is important to note. In your walk of faith, you might encounter a similar experience. Perhaps you have already experienced it. You may live right, practice obedience, and spend time with God on a regular basis only to have people still mistreat you. It is not uncommon for the people around you to project their insecurity onto you because they want to be in your same position.

Just like they did with Daniel, they'll talk about you and even make plans to kill you—maybe not physically, but most definitely spiritually. But Daniel's response is key. When he found out about the king's decree, he went right back to his room with open windows and prayed three times a day. He even thanked God! He chose to fix His eyes on Jesus and continue to do what he had been doing along. Nothing changed for him.

In our day and age, this would be similar to him going on Facebook live to show the world that he would continue to pray. It would be like posting on Instagram three times a day to remind everyone that God is most important to him. Daniel made it his priority to communicate with God on a daily basis, even if it would cost him his life.

It makes sense. When you are deeply in love, you want to tell the whole world. You need everyone to know how you feel and you don't care who knows! I think it's safe to say that Daniel wanted his relationship with God to be on display. Not for prideful reasons, but because His relationship with God meant everything to Him.

Here's the kicker, though: because Daniel was obedient and committed to God, God was able to get the glory. God protected him in the lions' den, and this caused the king to make a new decree, a decree requiring the entire kingdom to worship and serve the true and living God.

Action Item/Reflection:

1. What are your thoughts on Daniel 6? Can you relate to Daniel?

2. Even if it cost you, would you continue to communicate with God on a regular basis? What will it take for you to reach this type of commitment?

WEEK 2 REFLECTION

How did week 2 go? Reflect on this past week and record what you learned about communicating with God. How did your prayer life change? How do you feel the Holy Spirit spoke to you through God's Word? Write down any observations.

ADDRESSING DISCONTENTMENT AND HABITUAL SIN

ADDRESSING DISCONTENTMENT AND HABITUAL SIN

This week, we are adding another piece to the necklace—allowing the Lord to identify areas of discontentment and habitual sin in our hearts and lives. We hope you can see how everything is connected. Prioritizing time with Jesus leads to better communication with Him, which then allows Him the chance to address habitual sin and areas of discontentment.

DISCONTENTMENT AND HABITUAL SIN IN A RELATIONSHIP

Now, the topics of discontentment and habitual sin are sensitive ones. But the keys to overcoming both are abiding in God's love for you, confessing it before God, and using transparency and openness within a community that you trust.

When you root your identity in Christ knowing that He stands in your place, you can overcome the guilt. Open transparency and confession of sin bring forgiveness and the true freedom to experience the fullness of joy that Christ has granted (James 5:16).

In a romantic relationship, discontentment and sin can cause distance and mistrust. They become amplified! Think about it. If you are in a romantic relationship and are dealing with an unconfessed, habitual sin, your sin directly affects your partner. They will have to bear the consequences of your sin, and it will hurt them.

The same goes for discontentment. Depending on your partner to fill your needs is not sustainable. When you put pressure on him or her to listen, act, and feel the way YOU want them to, your relationship becomes unhealthy. Only Christ can fill those deepest voids.

And truth be told, these same concepts apply to your relationship with Christ no matter what your marital status is. Sin and discontentment drive you further away from Him.

DEALING WITH DISCONTMENT AND HABITUAL SIN

You must bring all sins and feelings of discontentment to Christ. Surrendering your all starts with loving God with all your heart, soul, and mind (Matthew 22).

In a sermon titled "Loving God," the speaker says something so profound. "A relationship with Christ is the only relationship in which you never have to guard your heart."

That is HUGE!

Your partner or community cannot bear the consequences of your sins, and they cannot solve your problems of discontentment. You will ALWAYS have to guard your heart and emotions with people. But in a relationship with Christ, you can openly confess and invite Him into every area of your life without fear.

Living in the bondage of sin and discontentment is not the life

God has called us to. He has called us to be rooted and secure in Him so that we might live life with joy. Joy is different from happiness because happiness lasts for a short period and it is contingent on our earthly circumstances. But joy is a fruit of the spirit.

Joy, gifted to us by the Holy Spirit and through abiding in Jesus, allows us to withstand any trial or heartbreak with confidence in the steadfast love of Christ. His steadfast love compelled Him to go to the cross, and that same love will lead us through this life until eternity.

When we trust in His steadfast love, we can be assured that all things will work together for our good because we love Him and have surrendered our lives to Him (Romans 8:28).

We encourage you to do the following this week:

1. Ask the Lord to identify areas of discontentment and expose habitual sins in your life.
2. Once you've identified these areas, **confess** them to the Lord.
3. Identify 1–2 accountability partners that you trust and confess your sins and challenges to them this week. Take it deeper and establish plans to be accountable frequently. This could be weekly or biweekly moving forward.
4. Allow Jesus to speak to those areas, heal, and have control of your life and heart.
5. Document any practical steps and advice that you receive from the Lord or your accountability partner(s) on fighting sin and discontentment.
6. Ask Christ to reveal to you how you can have joy despite areas where you may feel discontent, and to remind you of your identity in Him, as blameless and whole.

WEEK 3 RESOURCES

1. Loving God (a sermon)
2. How to Love God (a sermon)
3. Francis Chan's Daily Fight for Joy (a blog post)
4. 4 Signs You've Made Your Boyfriend an Idol (a blog post)
5. Falling Short: Battling Habitual Sin (a blog post)
6. Overcoming Sin & Shame (a blog post)
7. God's Love Language (a podcast)
8. Love to the Uttermost Devotional
9. #TheConfessionsProject Weekly Devotional
10. Stronger than the Struggle by Havilah Cunnington
11. Calm My Anxious Heart: A Woman's Guide to Contentment by Linda Dillow
12. Crazy Love: Overwhelmed by a Relentless God by Francis Chan
13. 4 Tips for Better Self-Confidence (a blog post)

DAY 15 - 1 JOHN 4:9–19

Sin can be challenging to understand, and harder to overcome. But from our own experiences, we've come to learn more about God, His grace, and His love for us as people. If you're struggling with a habitual sin, or the shame that the enemy uses to keep us in sin, know first and foremost that **God loves you so much**! He loves you more than you'll ever comprehend. He hates the sin but He LOVES you. When He looks at you, He doesn't see sin. He sees Jesus because Christ took residence inside your heart when you received salvation.

He willingly decided to take your place. He became flesh so that your relationship with God could be restored. God wouldn't have sent His son to die on the cross unless He thought that you were worth it. The complete opposite is true. God sent His son because He didn't want a world without YOU.

So when you sin, no matter how often, God wants you to come to Him. We can't allow shame to prevent us from approaching the throne and asking God for forgiveness. Failure to do this is a clear indication that we don't understand the power of the gospel or the beauty of the cross.

Sin only brings confusion. Just like Adam and Eve who tried to make fig leaves and cover themselves after they sinned, sin makes us think that we must make a covering for ourselves and find provision outside of God's will. So you spend more time with your significant other or spouse rather than God. You cover yourself with the pleasure of sexual impurity rather than the righteousness of the Holy Spirit. You turn to the comfort of food or substances rather the comfort of Christ.

It's why you feel like you can't turn to God. It's why you can't bear to go to church because you feel so unclean. You keep beating yourself up because you don't understand why you can't get it right. So you sin again. You find yourself in this never-ending cycle of sinning, and then sitting in shame, and then sinning once more. It's why some pastoral leaders step down from their role in ministry because they feel unworthy. They fail to realize that God's grace is sufficient.

I'm not saying that sin doesn't have consequences. "The wages of sin is death (Romans 6:23, NIV)," but don't fall into the trap of the enemy by thinking you're too far from God's reach. That thought or seed of doubt is not from God.

The truth is we were never really "deserving," but Jesus died anyways while we were STILL sinners (Romans 5:8). God is merciful and gracious. Matthew 9:36, NLT, says,

"When he saw the crowds, he had compassion on them because they were confused and helpless, like sheep without a shepherd."

God is also full of compassion. When you humble yourself and recognize your need for healing, redemption, and deliverance, Jesus takes His rightful role as Savior. It says in Luke 19:10, NLT,

"For the Son of Man came to seek and save those who are lost."

Let's be clear: God is displeased with your sin, but He does not sit there in heaven and condemn you. John 3:17 says, NLT, "God sent his Son into the world not to judge the world, but to save the world through Him." Condemnation is not His strategy.

True freedom from sin comes from spending time with God in His presence. Do use wisdom when you are battling a severe addiction or mental health condition and know when to seek professional help, but many Christians who are struggling with sin should repent, which is to turn away from their sin and turn towards God.

The greatest thing about God is that He is alive. When you spend time with Him on a consistent basis, you encounter His love for you. You encounter His grace. He brings living water and refreshes your soul. He fills your empty voids. He gives you peace and hope. He changes your entire life.

He goes even further and helps you sort your emotions. He enables you to process things, and if you sit long enough, He takes you through a healing process. But **the whole time** He loves you harder. He loves you deeper. He leads by example when demonstrating 1 Peter 4:8, NIV, where it says, "Above all, love each other deeply because love covers a multitude of sins."

Know that God's love is not an excuse to keep sinning, but there is FULL redemption in Jesus Christ! As you grow in Him and learn your identity, there comes a point when you respond to His encounter by turning from your ways. You begin to obey His commandments—not out of obligation but out of honor. You live by His standards out of reverence and respect for His sovereignty. You start to trust that His plan for your life is better than what you could come up with on your own.

There's no pressure to be perfect. He said that His yoke is easy and His burden is light (Matthew 11:30). You won't always get it right, but God calls you His beloved. So allow yourself to be loved. Seek Him wholeheartedly and know that when you seek Him, you will find Him (Jeremiah 29:13).

It won't be easy. In fact, it'll probably be one of the hardest things you ever have to overcome. But the enemy will attack where you are purposed. He'll use generational curses to stop you from accomplishing what you're destined to do here on this earth. Thankfully, you already have the victory! You can take heart because God has overcome (John 16:33). And greater is He that is in You than he that is in the world (1 John 4:4).

Action Item/Reflection:

1. After reading these thoughts, do you think you have a faulty view of God's love towards you? What do you think that view is?

2. How can you remind yourself of God's love especially if you're battling with shame?

DAY 16 - ROMANS 8

Imagine this picture: you are standing before God, the Father, and in His hand is a long scroll listing every sin that you have ever committed. You can expect for Him to send you to hell right now, but Jesus steps in front of you, places Himself before you and the Father, and says,

"No, Dad, you cannot condemn [insert your name here] because you already sent me to the cross. Remember? You and I agreed before time that I was going to go to earth and die for the sins of the world. Remember when you abandoned me in the garden when I cried tears of blood? Remember the moment when I was nailed to the cross? Remember that?"

Then God responds, "True. I mean I was there too because if you think about it We are one, so I technically turned myself into human form, came to earth, and died. I abandoned myself for [] too. It was my doing. I did it because I love [] and desired to be reconciled with her. Thanks for reminding me, Son."

He then turns to you and says, "[], I'm taking my blood and putting a big fat XXX on this scroll because your debt has been paid in full. There is no condemnation for you. Whatever you need, ask in my name because you are now part of the family. Now go proclaim my name."

Wow, friend. This is precisely what Jesus did for us. When sin wanted to condemn us, Jesus condemned sin on our behalf by living the perfect life that we could not live and dying the death that we deserved. Because of the work that He did for us, we are no longer slaves to sin. We have the Holy Spirit to help and guide us.

We have direct access to the Spirit. He lives in us, leads us through conviction, and is coaching us through our day-to-day life. As if that was not enough, these verses encourage us that we have a greater hope in eternity although our present body and flesh may fail us at times. We have a greater hope in a day and place where sin will no longer exist.

This verse reminds us that we live in a fallen world, and we are not immune to sin or evil. However, the Word promises us that we will overcome and absolutely nothing will separate us from the love of God. If this isn't the most comforting verse in the Bible, I am not sure what is! What sin are you dealing with? Are you feeling condemned, hopeless, tired of fighting sin and discontentment?

Whatever it is, reread these verses and let it sink in that God knows you and sees you where you are today. Hold on to these verses because He promises that He has and will continue to overcome for you. He has a greater hope for you and promises that you will be victorious because you are His child.

Action Item/ Reflection:

1. What events/areas have caused you to feel separated or distant from God? How do these verses speak to that lie? Write it down.

2. How do you feel that hope in future glory will help you fight sin and combat discontentment in your present body?

DAY 17 - PHILIPPIANS 4

Discontentment is a word that is thrown around a lot, wouldn't you agree? It seems many people struggle with it and maybe you're one of them, but what exactly does discontentment mean? Naturally I looked it up, and contentment is defined as a state of happiness or satisfaction.

Spiritually, I think this means to have a sense of peace and joy, especially when it comes to knowing who you are and Who you belong to. But it is also a battle between the flesh and spirit (see Galatians 5:17–19), and it is nothing but an identity crisis.

A good friend put it this way: have you ever been to a symphony or heard an orchestra play? Or maybe you played an instrument growing up. When you miss a key or when someone is offbeat or out of tune, it's noticeable. It doesn't sound right, and this is exactly what discontentment does with our hearts.

Discontentment prevents you from tapping into who God created you to be. When you are out of alignment—meaning you are discontent in areas of your life like your finances, your health, your relationships, or your purpose—it is often because your identity is rooted in something else.

We cannot confuse the provision with the Supplier. God is our source, and it is He who will supply every single one of our needs (Philippians 4:19). If we think that a new job or a new relationship or a new body will satisfy us, we've completely failed in our understanding of where our joy and satisfaction comes from. That's why many people get married or get jobs and still struggle with being content. We cannot experience anything greater than the fullness God gives. C.S. Lewis put it best,

"So if God loves us enough to make our joy full, he must win from us the praises of our hearts—not because he needs to shore up some weakness in himself or compensate for some deficiency, but because he loves us and seeks the fullness of our joy that can be found only in knowing and praising Him, the most magnificent of all beings.

God is the one Being in all the universe for whom seeking His own praise is the ultimate loving act. For him, self-exaltation is the highest virtue. When he does all things 'for the praise of his glory,' he preserves for us and offers to us the only thing in all the world that can satisfy our longings."

God is the only one who can quench that thirst for significance or purpose. Maybe you struggle with comparison? You look at the woman next to you to see what she is doing. Maybe your identity is in your performance? Or maybe you struggle with the fear of man?

These insecurities are the result of not knowing who you are. When you understand AND believe that you belong to God and He deeply loves you, you won't feel like you have to prove yourself to other people constantly. You won't have to compromise what's pleasing to God for what's popular. You can rest in knowing that God is using your uncomfortable season to prepare you for what He has for you. His perfect love casts out all fear (1 John 4:18)—the fear that you don't fit in, the fear that you'll never be good enough, the fear that people will reject you, or the fear that your life will be insignificant.

It's human nature to care about what other people think, but I'm reminded of one of my favorite quotes by Elizabeth Alves, who said,

"The fear of man is our greatest detriment to knowing and serving God. Only as we lay down our worries about what people think of us and what to expect of others can God honestly and openly speak into our lives."

We must learn to give God complete control of our lives. We must learn to place our identity in Him.

"When difficult circumstances come into my life, I hear God's voice saying, 'Let Me be the Blessed Controller. Surrender. Accept my timing. Accept my ways. Accept my outcome. Let your trust be in Me alone.' His voice also says, 'Make secret choices that will honor Me. Though no one sees your choices or knows how difficult they are, make them for Me.'"

- Linda Dillow, Calm My Anxious Heart

If God is Lord of your life, if He is the center—when you know who you are—you won't struggle with being discontent. This is easier said than done, but despite anything you are going through, know that you are chosen as a daughter or son of the Most High. Christ lives on the inside of you, and you have access to every spiritual blessing He can give—blessings that are richer, rarer, and more secure.

You were not qualified when you received salvation and the Holy Spirit, but God still willingly decided to be your portion. Is that enough for you today? Even when your soul knows He is enough, but your flesh does not feel it, will you continue to thank God for His grace?

Action Item/Reflection:

1. What areas of your life are causing you to be discontent? In those same areas, do you think you have placed your identity in them whether it be your performance, your job, your relationship, etc.?

2. Write a prayer asking God to help you give Him control over your life and the areas that you are discontent.

DAY 18 - JAMES 1:13–15

"Satan tempts. God tries. But the same trial may be both a temptation and a trial, and it may be a trial from God's side, and a temptation from Satan's side, just as Job suffered from Satan, and it was a temptation; but he also suffered from God through Satan, and so it was a trial to him."

(Spurgeon)

For many of us, the concept of this verse is tough to grasp. Some of us read this verse and instantly disagree, because how can a God, who is good, purposefully allow trials that can tempt us?

Why did He create plants that we are not allowed to smoke? We are sexual beings with sexual urges. Why can't we have sex outside of marriage? Like, what if someone is not married until the age of fifty, why can't they have sex? Let's take it back to Adam and Eve. If God is all-knowing and He knew Adam and Eve would eat from the tree anyway, why did He put the tree there in the first place?

There is one popular response to these questions, which is: God did not create us to be robots. He created us to be humans who are intellectual, possess judgment, and able to make their own decisions. His hope and desire are that despite the pressures of this world, we would still choose Him no matter what.

This verse states WHO God is and what He does NOT do—tempt us. It does a superb job of knocking us off our high horse, attacking our entitlement and "know it all" mentality, and telling us a story we have never heard. We are full of mess and sin. Period.

We might consider asking a different set of questions. Why are we so stubbornly sinful? Why do we act like we don't know right from wrong when our heavenly Father was clear in communicating these boundaries? Why are we prone to wander and rebel? Why do we believe a lie that God is always trying to withhold something from us, whether it is the tree, sex (because we all have needs) or drugs (because we need it to be stable)? The list goes on.

Listen: we have all been in situations when the line between a trial and temptation is blurred. But here is what we must consider before we blame God for our temptations next time.

1. *An enemy exists.*

His name is Satan. His only objective is to steal, kill, and destroy you (John 10:10). He is a deceiver, a liar, and a counterfeit, meaning that anything God intends to use to grow and sanctify us, Satan will thwart with the intention of hurting us. God uses trials to grow us. Satan tempts us in our trials when we are most vulnerable.

2. *We are sinful and ignorant.*

As stated above, we are self-centered. Adam and Eve had the whole garden and so much purpose. But because they felt like God was keeping something from them, they fell into the serpent's trap. Satan is not original AT ALL. He still uses this strategy today and sometimes we make the job too easy for him.

We, in our hearts, believe the lies. He just attacks when we are most vulnerable, and he uses those lies to tempt and destroy us. He is honestly not that powerful. He just knows our weaknesses. Seriously, Adam and Eve went down like that because of ONE TREE? ONE? In spite of the WHOLE GARDEN?

This is why it is so important to spend time with God and in the Word. In doing this, we begin to detect which thoughts are lies vs. which thoughts align with God's truth. By spending time with God, you start to recognize His voice so that you will be able to take every illegitimate thought captive and submit it to the obedience of Jesus Christ. Do not allow yourself to perish from a lack of knowledge (Hosea 4:6). Do not let ignorance to darken your understanding and separate you from God (Ephesians 4:18).

Seek God's wisdom and meditate on His Word both day and night. Hide His Word in your heart so that you don't sin against Him (Psalm 119:11). If you need help in this area, we encourage you to go back through Week 2 and dig into the resources provided.

3. Temptations and trials are two different outcomes, from beings with two different motives.

What this means is that what God intends for your good, the devil desires for your downfall. For example, let's talk about sex. Something SO good created by God for marriage, for pleasure, and to multiply the earth the devil has thwarted and used to destroy people's desires, their relationships, their life and plans, and marriages.

You see how that works? Maybe you are in a committed relationship, and the both of you are aiming to honor God and save sex for marriage. Waiting to have sex may seem like a trial. But in the end, waiting teaches you self-control and how to see your partner more than as flesh. It allows the chance for growth. It protects you from unplanned pregnancy, STDs, etc. But the devil uses your desire to tempt you.

The point is let us recognize that God is good, His plans for us are wonderful, and He wants to prosper us rather than hurt or deprive us.

Whatever habitual sin you are dealing with, take some time to think about what role you are playing in your temptation. Ask God to be the Lord of that area.

Action Item/Reflection:

1. What habitual sin or area of discontentment have you been battling and what lies have you believed concerning them?

2. In regards to what you are struggling with, what are you taking responsibility for?

DAY 19 - MARK 7:1–23

In these verses, we see that the Pharisees (an ancient Jewish sect known for a rigid observance of Jewish laws and traditions) condemn Jesus's disciples for eating with defiled hands, as in hands that were not washed before eating.

Now, can we just take a moment to recognize the level of pettiness here? We get it. We should wash our hands before we eat, but really? They really tried to come for Jesus's disciples like that? Okay, sorry; back to the devotional! Jesus, of course, is quick to defend His disciples and in doing so, He addresses the issue of the human heart.

Legalism

The first sin Jesus addresses is legalism, honoring God with external actions but not with our hearts. Anyone can be legalistic. It may look like attending church regularly, serving in the church, reading your Bible daily, attending Bible study, or going on a mission trip (all seemingly good things).

But if you are doing those things to impress other people, to abide by Christian culture, or to appease those who might be pressuring you to be a Christian, you are not genuinely honoring God with your heart.

If you are doing all of those "good and holy" things but behind closed doors, you are dealing with unconfessed sins or living a completely different lifestyle that is of the world, then you are serving God externally but not with your heart.

God would rather us be hot or cold, not lukewarm (Revelation 3:16). That is a scary place to be because Jesus says in the Bible that He will reject those who have led legalistic lives upon His return. Matthew 7:22–23, ESV, says,

21. Not everyone who says to me, 'Lord, Lord,' will enter the kingdom of heaven, but the one who does the will of my Father who is in heaven.

22. On that day many will say to me, 'Lord, Lord, did we not prophesy in your name, and cast out demons in your name, and do many mighty works in your name?'

23. And then will I declare to them, 'I never knew you; depart from me, you workers of lawlessness.'

Traditions of Man

The next thing Jesus addressed is how the teachings of the Pharisees reflect the teachings of man, not of God. The example given in this particular text describes a Jewish law in which funds initially used to care for one's parents were declared Corban, dedicated to God.

This meant that people were no longer obligated to care for their parents, which went against the commandment to honor our parents and care for those in need. How many of us have tried to twist God's words and commandments to benefit us or circumvent responsibility?

For example, maybe you've seen churches use the gospel to push their agenda. Or perhaps you've taken scripture outside of context or abused God's grace as an excuse to do what's more convenient and comfortable. Whatever it is, we must be careful to avoid these behaviors. Otherwise, our lives will reflect that of the Pharisees too.

Living based on religion rather than out of a relationship with God will harden our hearts, cause us to live in disobedience, and ultimately cause us to miss out on what God has planned for our lives. When you begin to live based on the traditions of man, your heart and motives will become impure. You will start to live based on your performance rather than resting in the love God has for you. But God asks us to love Him with our whole heart, soul, mind, and strength (Luke 10:27).

What Defiles a Man

Jesus then tells the Pharisees that nothing that goes into the body can defile the body because whatever goes into the body, such as defiled food, will go to the stomach and eventually exit as waste. Jesus says that what comes out of a person is what defiles them. Because things that come out of a person are a reflection of what is in their heart.

The human heart is sinful: sexual immorality, theft, murder, adultery, greed, malice, deceit, lewdness, envy, slander, arrogance, and folly (Mark 7:22). All these evils come from the inside and can defile a person. May we submit to you that on the flip side nothing done externally can save us, make us more holy, or deserving of God's grace?

Jesus then declares all food clean for these reasons because the only reason why He made the distinction between clean and unclean food was to highlight how holy and pure God is and how unclean we are. Moreover, it was there to highlight how our sin separates us from God and what is needed for us to have access to His presence. But the real issue, even from the beginning of time, was an issue of the human heart.

Because Jesus was able to address the issue of the sinful heart, He declared all food clean. The idea is that once He resolved the subject of the human heart, we could have fellowship with God, freely. It is for freedom's sake that Christ set us free from the law (Galatians 5:1). We no longer have to be slaves to the law, we are sons and daughters of God.

Now, what does all of that have to do with habitual sin and discontentment? These verses highlight the core issue, our hearts. For example, you may be discontent because you believe the lie that God is withholding a good thing from you, when in fact the Word says, "No good thing does He withhold from those who walk uprightly (Psalm 84:11, ESV)." In that situation, God is either protecting you or perhaps He is still maturing you so that you can receive what He has. Or maybe you are dealing with habitual sin because you are living in darkness and isolation.

Ultimately, when we see discontentment and sin displayed in our lives, they are the fruit of what is in our hearts. But let us encourage you, you are not a slave! Jesus redeemed you because of what He finished on the cross! He lives on the inside of you and stands in your place as the atoning sacrifice you need to be reconciled with God. So ask God to cleanse you of your sins and pray that He would help you! Like David said in Psalm 139:23–24, NIV,

23. Search me, God, and know my heart; test me and know my anxious thoughts.
24. See if there is any offensive way in me, and lead me in the way everlasting.

Action Item/Reflection:

1. What are root problems in your heart causing you to deal with particular sin(s) that you are battling?

2. What do you think God is withholding from you right now? What does the Word say about this? Can you identify ways in which God might be protecting you or maturing you to receive what He has?

3. Can you identify areas where your sin may be hindering you from walking in the fullness of joy and light that God has called you to? Write them down here and pray that God would restore this joy to you.

DAY 20 - PSALM 16

Today, we will pull heavily from a book, called *Calm My Anxious Heart,* by Linda Dillow. It is a twelve-week bible study and a woman's guide to finding and understanding what it means to be content. We highly recommend that you purchase this book if you can.

> *"I know of no greater simplifier for all of life. Whatever happens is assigned. Does the intellect balk at that? Can we say that there are things that happen to us that do not belong to our lovingly assigned 'portion' ("This belongs to it; that does not")?*
>
> *Are some things, then, out of the control of the Almighty? Every assignment is measured and controlled for my eternal good. As I accept that given portion other options are canceled. Decisions become much easier, directions clearer, and hence my heart becomes inexpressibly quieter (Psalm 16:5)"*
>
> *– Elisabeth Elliot*

We are not sure what it is that you are facing today, what you are discontent about or longing for. It may be a relationship, a marriage, a child, a new job, a career, admittance into professional school, or discovering your passions.

May we submit to you that the thing(s) you are longing for "later" will never satisfy you once you get them? The more we run after another god, our sorrows shall multiply (Psalm 16:4), and the joys of the here and now will slip through our fingers.

But, when Jesus is our chosen portion, we experience an unmatched joy. We experience contentment. We choose to be still because we know that He is Abba Father and steadfast. We know that He will never leave us.

When we keep our eyes fixed on the eternal work of salvation that He completed for us, we know that anything else we desire is a temporary and lesser thing. He went to the cross and defeated death for us. If He could do that, which was impossible for man, surely, the things we desire right now are only a small thing for Him.

Hear us though. Because Jesus died on the cross does not mean that your desires are insignificant. He asks us to freely cast our cares and make known our requests to Him. But with that comes this:

> *Fixing your eyes on eternity. Knowing that your tomorrow belongs to God, and because your tomorrow belongs to God, you can trust that whatever you lay at His feet are nestled in His strong arms. Knowing this, you can live freely today*
>
> — *Linda Dillow*

Today, declare that He is your chosen portion! As Elliot so beautifully said, trust that the lot He has allocated to you, whether it is singleness, another year out of school, at that job, inability to birth that child—whatever it is—trust that as long as you have surrendered your life to Him, where you are now is where He has called you to be. It is not a mistake; He is intentional. He is faithful to save and sanctify you.

As per usual, we want to acknowledge that contentment is hard. It's hard to be content when those around you seem to have the things you are longing for. It is hard to *feel* like Abba hasn't forgotten you. Sometimes, as a child of God, you can feel like the left-out middle child, to which God seems to be giving no attention at all.

It's difficult to cry tears that you feel nobody sees, tears that God does not see. Discontentment can make you feel isolated, so much so that you start to believe lies about God and doubt His immense love for you. But Dillow gives us a remedy:

How does God enable us to be content? He infuses contentment into us through His Word. As it seeps into our minds, it transforms us. Just as a cup of tea gets stronger when we give it time to steep, so we become more content when we spend time in God's Word and allow it to seep into our lives, transforming us to be like Him.

These may just seem like words, cliché even, but Friend, this is truth. The beautiful thing about the stories of the Bible is that the people in it never lived perfect lives. Think about Abram and Sarai, who did not see their promise of having a son until they were old. Think about Abel, who was pleasing to the Lord but was murdered by his brother Cain. Think of Paul, literally the OG of the Bible. He was persecuted for most of his life, especially when he wrote most of the New Testament.

But most importantly, think of Jesus, God Himself, the greatest man to walk on earth. He died on the cross for you. None of these people lived easy lives, but because of their steadfastness and unshakable faith, you now have access to their stories in the Bible. They had to go through the disappointments and trials so that you can be encouraged.

So if you're struggling, you're in good company. Be encouraged today that whatever you are facing is not a waste. It is the Lord's portion for you. Regardless of what it is He sees you, and He will use whatever it is that you are dealing with for your good and your growth.

Action Item/Reflection:

Today, we want you to pray this scripture over yourself:

Preserve me from the world, in YOU, not the things I am desiring. I trust you, God. My flesh may be weak, but my soul that will be with you in eternity SHOUTS that you are my LORD and apart from You, I have no good.

My spirit is willing to trust not fear, to be content, and to find Joy in this season. My flesh may not be there yet, but thank you, Lord, that where I am weak you are strong, and your grace is sufficient for me today and every day. Thank you, Lord, that you have lovingly assigned my lot. That you, oh God, are my portion.

DAY 21 - PSALM 139

Have you ever considered that there's a high possibility you're experiencing discontentment, shame, doubt, and anxiety simply because you decide to speak it over your life? Do you always talk about how things won't work out or complain that you're always frustrated?

Whether it's battling habitual sin or overcoming discontentment, we must be mindful of our tongue and be intentional about speaking life. We cannot let our mouths be our undoing, and we cannot allow our lips be the snare to our very life (Proverbs 18:7).

To take it one step further, you may *say* that God can keep you, but do you really believe He will? Do you believe He'll save you from your shame, put you back together, and lift your head high?

When I was younger, my mom enrolled me in an enrichment program that was hosted by my church where we would learn various topics: etiquette, African American history, computer skills, etc. Every Saturday, my mother would make sure I put on my uniform and report to church. And every Saturday, we were required to repeat this call and response titled, "I Am Somebody."

They were written by and based on Psalm 139. They are as followed.

I Am Somebody

I am somebody that God loves, provides for, and protects.

For you created my innermost being. You knit me together in my mother's womb.

I am a marvelous work of art. The color of my eyes, the texture of my hair, the features of my face, the shape of my body were all conceived and designed by the Creator of the universe.

I praise you because I am fearfully and wonderfully made. Your works are wonderful.

God himself took time to watch over me while my parts were being formed. The plans for my life were laid out before I was born.

My frame was not hidden from you when I was made in the secret place. When I was woven together in the depths of the earth, your eyes saw my unformed body. All the days ordained for me were written in your book before one of them came to be.

I am so important that God keeps track of the number of hairs on my head. He thinks of me constantly and plans for my good.

How precious to me are your thoughts, o God! How vast is the sum of them. Were I to count them, they would outnumber the grains of sand.

The God of the universe is my Creator.

I am Somebody.

I am precious in my Father's sight, protected by my Father's might. I am created by my Father's hand, destined by my Father's plan. Nurtured in my father's love, I am heir to earth and all above. I am Somebody.

If you are struggling with loving yourself or seeing yourself the way that God sees you, then I challenge you to take part in #TheConfessionsProject Challenge. Speaking God's Word out loud will help you overcome any problems you have with believing what He says about you. It activates your faith because it's one thing to speak God's truth, but you must receive and believe His word for it to take its effect in your life.

When you wake up every morning, repeat the words to "I Am Somebody" OUT LOUD before your feet even hit the ground. I challenge you to do this for at least thirty days even after you finish this devotional. And don't skip a day. These words still come back to encourage me even after all these years. They are empowering because you will go from doubting yourself to believing every single word that God says about you.

Action Item/Reflection:

1. Participate in #TheConfessionsProject Challenge if you are struggling to believe God's Word.

2. Find scripture in the Bible that speak to any situation you're currently facing and use them whenever life gets you down.

WEEK 3 REFLECTION

How did week 3 go? Reflect on this past week and record what you learned about yourself regarding habitual sin and areas of discontentment. Has your view changed on how you see yourself and how God sees you? Did you establish any accountability partners? Write down any observations.

GOING ON A DATE WITH JESUS

WEEK 4

DATING JESUS

This week we present to you our final challenge, and that is to go on a date with Jesus.

You may or may not be a bit intimidated by this, but hear us out. It's one thing to spend time with someone in a relationship, but it's another thing to set aside time to go on intentional dates! Are we right or are we right??

SO! Let's do the same with Jesus and set aside a special time with Him, the ULTIMATE BAE. And if you don't have an earthly bae, Jesus is waiting for you!

The challenge this week is simple if you don't overthink it. Go to a place you have never been before and do something special with Jesus. You have complete freedom in how you choose to do this. You can make it as fancy or as simple as you want. Think of a creative way to engage with Him.

Maybe that's finding a quiet place to write or searching the Word on a particular topic and asking that He will minister to you at that moment! Maybe you'll go to a restaurant and read your Bible over dinner. Perhaps you'll take a walk or go to a coffee shop. The biggest thing is to trust and expect that no matter what happens, God will honor that time with you.

To set you up for success, we'll be looking at the various characteristics of God throughout the week and how that looks within the context of a relationship. When you're dating someone, learning about their character never stops. People grow over time, so there is always something new to learn whether that's how they handle different situations or what their preferences are.

In the same way, let's position our hearts to learn more about God. Outside of going on your date with Jesus, take this week to learn about who He is rather than what He can do. Ask God to reveal Himself to you, and ask that He would allow you to see yourself the way that He sees you.

The thing about relationships is that you're always learning about each other—them about you and you about them. That doesn't stop once we enter into a relationship with Jesus. If anything, it's a better discovery process. You picked up this book because you want to learn what it means to be in a relationship with Christ. Let's continue to dive in and find out!

WEEK 4 RESOURCES

1. 5 Keys To Identifying Your SoulMate - Touré Roberts (a sermon and personal favorite—trust me, it is more than you think)
2. Dating Jesus: The Single Cure for Loneliness (a blog post)
3. Single, Satisfied and Sent (a blog post)
4. 25 Dates with God by Cheryl McKay
5. God's Character (a blog post)
6. How to Love God (a sermon)
7. Crazy Love: Overwhelmed by a Relentless God by Francis Chan

DAY 22 - EXODUS 20

JEALOUS

So God is a jealous God. The Bible tells us this and here is some proof:

- Exodus 20:5, NASB: You shall not worship them or serve them; for I, the LORD your God, am a jealous God, visiting the iniquity of the fathers on the children, on the third and the fourth generations of those who hate Me.
- Exodus 34:14, NASB: For you shall not worship any other god, for the LORD, whose name is Jealous, is a jealous God.
- Deuteronomy 4:24, NASB: For the LORD your God is a consuming fire, a jealous God.
- Deuteronomy 32:16, NASB: They made Him jealous with strange gods; with abominations they provoked Him to anger.
- Psalm 78:58, NASB: For they provoked Him with their high places and aroused His jealousy with their graven images.

Okay, we are done spamming you with scripture. But wait. Can we just take a moment of silence for the Israelites in Deuteronomy and Exodus? Why were they ALWAYS in trouble with God though? Like, how many times did He have to tell these folks "I AM A JEALOUS GOD! GET YOUR LIVES TOGETHER." Literally, almost all verses about jealousy were from those two books, HAHA! Okay, let's get back on track!

Firstly, what does the jealousy of God even mean? According to the ESV Study Bible,

"God the Creator is worthy of all honor from his creation. Indeed, his creatures (mankind esp.) are functioning properly only when they give God the honor and worship that He deserves. God's jealousy is therefore also his zeal for his creatures' well-being."

Let's break this down.

1. God is jealous for us because He carefully and intentionally created us in His image.

God is jealous for us because He created us in His image, to be holy and blameless before Him. This was His original intent. So when we step outside of the character He has called us to, there is righteous jealousy that rises in Him.

Think about it this way: if you created something, anything, and designed it to do a certain thing or behave a certain way, how would you feel if it did the exact opposite of what you intended for it to do? How happy would you be? Not very happy, we are sure.

How about this? Let's say you have a child and your child seems to be cold towards you, but when they see a stranger, they run to them with excitement. Wouldn't you be hurt? You would probably say to your child "I birthed you, clothe you, provide for you. I try to love you and show you that I am here for you, and you can't even look me in the eyes but will run with open arms to a total stranger?"

Righteous anger and jealousy would rise in your spirit because you love your child and desire for them to love you in return. This is how God feels when we run after other gods, have idols, or even run to other people for advice before Him. He is jealous for us because He loves us.

2. We were bought with a price.

Another reason why God is jealous for us is because He died for us. He died to have us. But how often do we forget this and rebel against Him?

> *For you have been bought with a price: therefore glorify God in your body.*
>
> 1 CORINTHIANS *6:20, NASB*

It was not cheap for Jesus to go to the cross for us. It cost the Father everything to abandon and send His blameless son, Jesus. Can you imagine how He felt when Jesus was crying tears of agony to the point of sweating blood in the Garden of Gethsemane?

Can you imagine how it felt to look down on His son crying and saying, "Father, I know we decided that I would die on the cross before time, but it's going to be hard. Is there another way? Please don't forsake me," and then to abandon Him? Can you even fathom what it felt like for Him to see His son nailed to the cross, taking on the disgusting sin and shame of the world?

It was painful for God, but He did it because He was jealous for us and wanted us *that* badly. He did it because He wanted us to be reconciled with Him, to go back to our first love, to be holy and blameless before Him again.

Can you put yourself in God's shoes for a second? His LOVE for you makes him righteously jealous for you. If He did not care about you, your sin would not anger Him. Why? He did everything possible to save your life to have you in eternity with Him. So sin angers Him and makes Him jealous because He knows that sin will separate you from Him and He wants you close.

Think about it practically. If you are in a romantic relationship, you are jealous for that person, so much so that when they hurt you, it hurts badly. Why? You have such a strong connection to that person and care so badly and deeply for them. When they hurt, you hurt too. You even become jealous at the thought of them being with another person. Would you go to the cross for your boyfriend, girlfriend, wife, or husband?

We are not sure, but what we know is that Jesus went to the cross because He was THAT jealous for you. He was able to risk it all for you! Let's reflect on that today.

Action Item/Reflection:

1. Have you recently stepped outside of the character God designed for you?

2. What do you need to repent of today?

DAY 23 - ISAIAH 55

INTELLIGENT

Have you ever had a stimulating conversation with someone and was immediately turned on by their brilliance? Or maybe you date, or you're married to someone who's so smart! So smart that every time they demonstrate their creativity or their skills, you are amazed by their genius? Or they know how to communicate and express their thoughts in a way that it leaves you stunned?

The crazy part about God is that He goes above and beyond all that. He is the ultimate craftsman, and there's nothing that He can't do. I mean think about physics, chemistry, biology. Those subject are difficult unless you're a genius, right? Or maybe that's just us, but God used all of them to create the entire universe!

Let's make it more personal. Think about your own life. God has it all planned out, even to the last detail. This still holds true whether you believe it or not. He picked the best version for your life and knew exactly what you need to continue in the plan that He has for you, plans to prosper you, give you hope, and a future (Jeremiah 29:11). He is the master strategist.

The bottom line I'm trying to make is that God is intelligent. Not only is He intelligent, but He is also wise. Intelligence is the ability to acquire and apply knowledge and skills, but wisdom is the quality of having experience and good judgment. Verses 8 and 9 in Isaiah 55 (NIV) say,

> 8 *"For my thoughts are not your thoughts, neither are your ways my ways," declares the Lord.*
> 9 *"As the heavens are higher than the earth, so are my ways higher than your ways and my thoughts than your thoughts.*

Can you imagine? But I also love 1 Corinthians 1:25, NIV, where it says,

For the foolishness of God is wiser than human wisdom, and the weakness of God is stronger than human strength.

But here's the kicker! This same intelligent and wise God whom I just talked about. Not only does He have the utmost compassion and love towards you, but He lives on the inside of you! He has taken residence inside your heart. That is why you're able to declare that you have the mind of Christ boldly.

You don't have to willingly live in anxiety and stress. You can still have your peace and joy because He holds your life in the palm of His hands, AND He has given you access to Him. Access to use His name to fight any temptation or lie from the enemy. We're so thankful He's smart and knows what He's doing!

Action Item/Reflection:

1. Take a moment to reflect on God's wisdom and intelligence. What do you think that means for you?

2. How can you take what you have read and apply it to your own life? What action steps can you take based on what you learned?

DAY 24 - JOHN 14

HONEST

We're back in John 14 again! Isn't it amazing how the same passage of scripture can pull out a ton of different revelations? We're sharing another characteristic of Jesus and this one deals with His character of honesty and truth.

When it comes to dating, there is nothing worse than being with someone who is a liar. If you've ever dated someone who is dishonest, you know how quickly that relationship will fall apart. Dishonesty can be one of the greatest problems within a relationship because right outside of communication, trust is vital.

When we look at who Jesus is, we see Him as nothing but honest. If anything, Jesus was too honest! Many times, we catch Him putting the disciples in their place because they didn't fully understand how the whole death and being raised to life was supposed to work. They may have known who Jesus was, but they didn't fully comprehend why Jesus was sent to earth. Like when Jesus rebukes Peter and even calls him Satan because Peter didn't want Jesus to die on the cross. (See Mark 8:33).

The thing about Jesus is that not only is He honest, but He is truth itself. I mean even the Word He speaks is true! That's how creation came into existence because God's Word could not return void to Him (Isaiah 55:11). Can you imagine that type of honesty? That everything in this world must submit to you because what you speak is true?

This means that the life Jesus lived was truth, the words He spoke were truth, and the gospels all give an account to this testimony that

Jesus lived. Jesus's life is what made the old scriptures true. Over and over we see Jesus telling his disciples that He would be raised to life.

I mean look at these verses right here in John 14. He's telling them how He's going to go back to heaven to prepare mansions for them. Jesus came to earth to live in truth and fulfill the law that was written before His coming. I love these verses in Matthew 5:17–19, NIV, where it says,

> 17 *"Do not think that I have come to abolish the Law or the Prophets; I have not come to abolish them but to fulfill them.*
> 18 *For truly, I say to you, until heaven and earth pass away, not an iota, not a dot, will pass from the Law until all is accomplished.*
> 19 *Therefore whoever relaxes one of the least of these commandments and teaches others to do the same will be called least in the kingdom of heaven, but whoever does them and teaches them will be called great in the kingdom of heaven.*

So why does all of this matter? We must follow God's example. We are called to be like Him because He is the way, the truth, and the life (verse 6). Just like Jesus went to the cross, we must crucify ourselves with Christ (see Galatians 5:24) and die to our flesh so that His will may be fulfilled. Or when lies from the enemy tempt us to believe that we're not good enough, we can take God's truth and hide it in our hearts. Clinging to God's truth and His ways is part of the purification process, and this spiritual development is what will help us stay the path as God continues to work in and through our lives.

Action Item/Reflection:

1. What ways do you think you can become more like Christ in your own life?

2. What stood out to you in John 14?

DAY 25 - EPHESIANS 3:14–19

LOVING

During the summer of 2014, I developed the BIGGEST crush on this guy. So much so that it made me feel deprived, like I was really lacking something in my life. As cliche as it sounds, I felt that if God gave me a boyfriend, life would be better.

I think the worst part was that this guy never knew that I had developed this crush on him, which ate me up inside. I had to keep all of my feelings contained from him and from people because I feared rejection. Furthermore, I was extremely insecure in myself and feared that what I had to offer and who I am was not good enough for others.

That summer was transformative for me because I worked through feelings of depravity with God. I asked God, "Why do I always develop these strong crushes on people?" He revealed to me the root of my discontentment in singleness through the illustration of a box.

He showed a picture of me holding a box, which housed all of my desires, dreams, wishes, a checklist of what I wanted in a spouse, and even my sin. In the picture, I was frantically walking around and longing to give this box to anyone who would take what I had to offer. In that season, I was specifically looking for a guy to take my box and fulfill my desires, affirm me, make me feel wanted, and good enough.

After God showed me this picture, He asked me to give Him that box. I struggled to give Him my box because at the core, I doubted His love for me and quite frankly did not understand just how deeply He loved me and what that looked like practically. I didn't know what God's love even meant, and I didnt see how it was enough to fulfill my desire for romantic love.

Towards the end of that summer, I read Ephesians 3: 14–19 and something clicked for me. God's love is so freaking wild, reckless, deep, wide, long, and all of the big words. I thought to myself, *Wow, Jemeia, it's hard for you to conceptualize God's love for you because it's so grand that you need supernatural strength to comprehend it.*

That is one of the reasons why Paul prayed that prayer. Because He understood that God's love is so complex to the point that he would never understand it. Additionally, because God loves you and me and sent His son, we have now inherited His spiritual gifts. Over the years, I have held on to two truths.

1. God's love is steadfast.

Psalm 136 reminds us of His steadfast love. This steadfast love compelled Jesus to go to the cross to save us. This faithful love is the Holy Spirit living inside of us. This steadfast love is God's dedication to pruning and sanctifying us until we stand before Him one day!

2. His love is eternal, so we need an eternal perspective.

Take some time to read Romans 8:28–30.

Because God is loving, we can conquer all things. We have a hope that is an anchor for our soul. We can trust that everything He allows us to walk through—the good, bad, even consequences for our sins—are filtered through His love. He will never intentionally hurt us, but He will go to great lengths to make us more like His Son.

We don't know what you are working on today, but we pray that at the very least you will trust that God loves you. We want to encourage you to take on an eternal perspective on life, which is to remember that nothing in this life lasts forever (good or bad). You are not a citizen of this earth. Your home is in heaven. Lift your eyes towards Him because He is where your help comes from (Psalm 121:2).

Action Items/Reflection:

Pray Ephesians 3 over yourself. Insert your name into the verses where possible.

1. Whatever you are facing today, how can you filter your situation through the lens of God's steadfast and eternal love?

2. Ask God to reveal His intention behind the situation you are facing today. Is He protecting you from something, teaching you patience, pruning you in a specific area, or just saying no or yes because He is your father and knows best?

3. Write down what God reveals to you on a sticky note and put it somewhere where you can remind yourself of truth the next time you start to doubt His love.

DAY 26 - NUMBERS 16

PERFECT AND HOLY

Prepare yourself because this Bible story is WILD! In this story, we see the true measure of God's perfection and holiness. When we think about Jesus, we don't think about him in this light, but His perfection and holiness is one of the only qualities that sets Him apart from us as people.

At this point in the story, the Israelites are pretty much fed up with Moses and all his shenanigans. They are tired of wandering around in the wilderness, and some of them don't think that Moses should even be the leader. They decide to take matters into their own hands. Three men by the names of Korah, Dathan, and Abiram are trying to stage a revolt, and they're able to get the support of 250 men. Mind you they are important leaders within the Israelite community.

Moses tries to work it out, but Korah, Dathan, and Abiram are not having it. And that's when Moses loses his temper and understandably goes to God to basically tell on them. He then lets everyone know that there will be a meeting between them and the Lord. And this is when things start to get crazy.

As soon as God shows up, He tells Moses and Aaron to step away from the leaders because he's legit about to smite them—all 250 of them. But when Moses and Aaron hear this, they fall face down and intercede for the people asking God to spare their lives. God obliges and asks them to step away from the tents of Korah, Dathan, and Abiram instead. (Note: You cannot tell us the Bible is not juicy!!)

Moses then allows God to prove who is rightfully in charge. He tells the people if Korah, Dathan, and Abiram are wrong, then they will be swallowed up by the ground. You read that right—swallowed by the ground! As soon as He says these words, God immediately opens up the ground taking Korah, Dathan, Abiram, their families, their children, and their belongings all with them. AND THEN God sends fire to consume the 250 men.

You would think the Israelites would have learned their lesson? Nope! The very next day, they complain and even blame Aaron and Moses for killing the Lord's people. God steps in again, and He is not playing anymore. He tells Aaron and Moses to step away as He sends a plague to kill the Israelites. Moses is pretty much panicking at this point and tells Aaron to offer a sacrifice, but by the time Aaron makes the atoning sacrifice, God has already killed 14,700 people. Think of your entire small hometown just GONE because of their rebellion.

This story is a demonstration of God's wrath in the purest form all because of His standard and character of righteousness and holiness. God is so holy that He cannot be where there is any form of sin—rebellion, dishonesty, pride, etc. It's why God had to abandon Jesus on the cross because Jesus took on the sins of the world.

This story in Numbers is a picture of the old covenant. God established a law, and the people of Israel agreed to it (Exodus 24). The contract was put in place between God and the people, and if there were any violations of the law, a high priest who was specifically called by God would repent and make an atoning sacrifice on behalf of the people. The people themselves couldn't even do this on their own; they had to depend on another person. It's also important to note that the atoning sacrifices didn't take away the people's sin. It was just a band-aid to appease God for violating His holy law.

But we read in Hebrews 10:9–10, NIV, that "Christ set aside the first [covenant] to establish the second." Through God's purpose, we have been made HOLY through the sacrifice of the body of Jesus Christ once and for all. "Sacrifice for sin is no longer necessary (verse 14)" because we have Jesus!

Christ lives inside you and on a regular basis stands in your place for your sin—the ones you know about and the ones you don't know anything about. Do you know how nuts that is? The same God who killed all those people in Numbers can extend grace towards you because of what Jesus did on the cross.

This is why it says in Matthew 5:17–20 that Christ came to fulfill the law. His death on the cross was the truest demonstration of His grace and mercy, and it's why scripture says we have been saved BY grace through faith (Ephesians 2:8–9). The gift of salvation is God's most precious gift to the world.

If you had a child who killed someone, you would understand if they had to go to jail. You would be heartbroken, but you would understand that they broke the law and now there is a consequence for their action. The laws in our government, although some may be unjust, have been put in place for a reason—to keep us safe.

God worked in the same way, but He is holy and perfect. He established a just law with the people that would keep them safe, but their sin came with consequences. Romans 6:23 says that the wages of sin is death. But because God loved us so much, He sent His only son to die on the cross for our sins (John 3:16).

That is a HUGE deal when you think about the type of consequences we deserve. If we're honest with ourselves, it's possible that we would have been one of the people killed if we were living during the revolt of Korah, Dathan, and Abiram. Let's take time to think about the weight of the gospel! We serve a holy and righteous God, but thank you Lord that He wanted a relationship with us so badly that He did whatever it cost to allow us to live in eternity with Him!

Action Items/Reflection:

1. Pray and thank God for your salvation. Reflect on everything Jesus has done for you and think about His amazing grace. Offer a prayer of thanksgiving to God.

DAY 27 - HEBREWS 4

RELATABLE

Our message to you today is yes, Jesus can relate.

Can Jesus relate to coming from a poor or imperfect family? Yes.

His mother, Mary, was a young virgin when she conceived Jesus by the power of the Holy Spirit. In fact, His father, Joseph, found out she was pregnant and considered ending the relationship because he thought that she had gotten pregnant out of wedlock. But an Angel appeared to Joseph and cleared things up and told him to marry Mary anyway (Matthew 1).

The beautiful part of this story is that God chose the seemingly weak. He used two people, a carpenter and young virgin woman, who were not highly regarded in society, and He used them to parent the Savior of the world.

Can Jesus relate to being human, living in a fallen world, and always being surrounded by evil and suffering? Yes.

Besides dying on the cross, Jesus came to touch the sick, poor, and broken. Every day He encountered people who needed physical and emotional healing, but more importantly a Savior. Before physically healing people, He would heal their hearts and address the issue of sin. To Him, making sure that their souls were saved was the most important thing (Mark 2:1–2)

Can Jesus relate to feeling abandoned, betrayed, and facing emotional and mental distress? Yes.

In the Garden of Gethsemane, biblical scholars believed that Jesus might have been crying tears of blood as He was asking the Father to withhold the ultimate cup of wrath from Him. Additionally, before going to pray in the garden, He asked His friends (His disciples) to keep watch for Him. Jesus finished praying only to find His disciples sleeping. Not only that, but one of His very own disciples, Judas, betrayed Him for a reward. Moreover, His disciple, Peter, denied knowing Him three times during the night that Jesus was arrested.

How many of us have denied or betrayed Jesus, whether it is in our hearts by justifying our sin or outwardly when we are ashamed to share the Gospel? We hope that as you think about Judas or Peter, you see yourself. Because all of us have denied and betrayed Jesus in our own way.

Can Jesus relate to facing temptations? Yes.

In Matthew 4, we see that Jesus was tempted by the devil after fasting for forty days and forty nights. Each time He was tempted by the devil, He responded with scripture and the tempter eventually fled. This not only shows you that Jesus is just like you and me, but He also modeled for us how we ought to respond when we are tempted. We are to use the LIVING WORD as a way to fight Satan and stand firm in our identity as holy and blameless before God.

Can Jesus relate to social/racial injustice and facing shame and guilt? Yes.

Look at the cross. Jesus was crucified alongside two criminals. They had obviously done something wrong, but Jesus did nothing wrong. He was lied on, betrayed by His friend, brutally beaten, crowned with thorns, forced to carry a cross on His back (all while being spat on and insulted by the masses watching Him carry His cross). He died nailed to the cross bearing the shame and guilt of this world for sins He never committed.

All while being wrongfully accused, He never once tried to defend Himself or use supernatural power to save Himself. He chose to be demeaned and wrongfully charged because of you. Because that was what He came to do. Save you.

Even in the midst of being betrayed and denied by His friends, He never once insulted them. He knew what Peter and Judas would do to Him at the last supper, but He never lashed out in anger. Instead, He washed their feet. Why? Because He is love and He had to be betrayed for His work to be completed here on earth.

Have you ever found yourself in a situation asking God, "Why did you have to put me through this? Why did you have to do things this way, God? Was there not another way, Lord?" Jesus can relate because He asked those very same questions. But had He not endured betrayal and pain "that way," you and I would not be saved.

Gosh, if you read that without getting emotional, I don't know what could be missing. In the world today, we see injustice in every form. We know of people who have been wrongfully accused of a crime and executed as a result. America suffers from the disease of mass incarceration, sex trafficking, poverty and hunger, and Jesus can relate to all of it because He was wrongfully punished for your sin.

We may not have covered every problem in the book, but we hope you can see that you do not serve a High Priest who cannot sympathize with suffering, pain, weakness, temptation, sickness, shame, guilt, a broken past, and broken family. You serve a God who was tempted in EVERY way. You serve a God who died on a cross, yet conquered death for you and overcame the world (Hebrews 4). That is the beauty of the gospel.

Action Items/Reflection:

1. In what areas of your life does Jesus relate to you? Write them here.

DAY 28 - GENESIS 3–4

JUST

A lot of people struggle with understanding that God is a just God, but God is just to punish sin, forgive sin, and cover us. He also has a heart of compassion for social justice.

Punishing Sin (Genesis 3)

God has always made His standards known to us from the beginning of time. When He created Adam and Eve, He gave them explicit instructions to care and tend to the garden. He specifically instructed them not to eat from the tree of knowledge of good and evil. When they disobeyed, He punished them accordingly.

His consequence for Eve was pain during childbirth, and He tells her this, *"Your desire shall be for your husband, and he shall rule over you."* His consequence to Adam was a hardship; nothing would come easy for him. Adam's original job was to tend to the garden. So the very thing He was created to do effortlessly would not be so effortless anymore because of his sin. Additionally, God sentenced Adam and Eve out of the garden, and the final punishment for the sins of the world was the death of Jesus.

Now before you question God, here is the thing: His punishment for sin was quite generous regarding the fact that Adam and Eve's sin was very serious. Their single decision brought sin into the world. Their disobedience is the reason why we all struggle with habitual sin and why there are so much evil and suffering. When they ate from that tree, it opened a door that allowed sin to take over this world.

God himself did not do that. WE did that. We say "WE" because if we read the story of Adam and Eve and don't see a reflection of ourselves, we are mistaken. God's punishment for Adam and Eve does not compare to the ultimate consequence, which is death (Romans 6:23).

Another thing to note regarding Eve's second punishment, which was her *desire shall be for her husband, and he shall rule over her,* is that God did not punish her, or women in general, in this way because He thought that men were superior to women or that women were inferior to men. Pastor Reggie Roberson, lead pastor of Kings Park International Church in Durham, NC, put it this way:

In marriage, men honor their wives by serving them and exhibiting a sacrificial love, as Jesus did for us. Women in return are to help their husbands live righteously, graciously allowing and helping them to lead the relationship. In other words, men are supposed to be willing to humble themselves to serve their wives and women have to be willing to humble themselves and allow their husbands to take leadership.

Because of sin, women and men are not able to see eye to eye, and instead of graciously submitting to their husbands, women desire to rule over them. Their husbands ruling over them sometimes causes strife. Hear us! This was NOT God's intention, but because of sin, we deal with these consequences.

Forgiving and Covering Sin (Genesis 3–4)

After explaining to Adam and Eve the consequences that they would face, God immediately kills an animal and uses its skin to cover their nakedness. This was foreshadowing of the sacrificial death of Jesus to cover the sins of the world.

In Genesis 4, He does the same with Cain. Adam and Eve have two sons, Cain and Abel. Cain kills his brother Abel, and God punishes Cain by telling him that while he will work the ground, it will not yield to him meaning he will work hard but bear no fruit. After accepting his punishment, Cain fears that someone else will kill him. The Lord promises Cain that anyone who kills him will receive vengeance that is sevenfold. Then the Lord puts a mark over Cain so that no one would attack him.

There are many examples in the Bible, but just within the first four chapters we see that God is not only just to punish sin, but He is also just to forgive sin and cover His children no matter how bad they mess up.

This was ultimately displayed on the cross. God's **sacrificial** love compelled Him to send His blameless Son (Himself in human form) to earth to die for our sins. When Jesus died, sin was punished and forgiven simultaneously.

If we confess our sins, He is faithful and just and will forgive us our sins and purify us from all unrighteousness.

1 JOHN 1:9, NIV

God is Passionate about Social Justice

God is passionate about social justice, and this is a major theme throughout the Gospels, particularly Luke. It was good news for sinners and those who were poor and marginalized by religious leaders. The Bible gives countless examples of God's heart for justice:

- He made all of mankind in His image and gave all of us dominion over the earth. Therefore, it is wrong for one group of people to have power over another. (Genesis 1:26–26, John 3:16)

Any form of injustice and hate (racial, ethical, religious, gender-based, economic) is not SIMPLY a sin problem that should be ignored and belittled. Using any of the categories mentioned above as an excuse for evil is weighty. It is a weight that Jesus himself felt when He endured shame and was condemned on the cross.

- Jesus was impartial and has called us also to be impartial. (Romans 2:11, James 2:4)
- When we act unjustly towards the marginalized, Jesus is impacted. (Matthew 25:40)

These are only a few examples of the types of injustices we face today, and some began at the beginning of creation. But what steps are are you taking to be more like Jesus? We hope that this devotional has encouraged you to forgive as God forgave you and to seek tangible ways that you can fight for justice in our fallen world. Our Jesus has the final say. He is sovereign and will return one day to end all injustice. But He has placed us on this earth for a reason. He has modeled justice for us. How will we respond?

Action Items/Reflections:

1. How have you seen God punish and forgive sins in your life?

2. What social issues are you passionate about? What steps are you taking to work towards social justice?

WEEK 4 REFLECTION

How did your date with Jesus go? Record your experience here. What have you learned about Jesus and His characteristics? What stood out to you? What's one of your favorites? Write down any observations.

NEXT STEPS

NEXT STEPS

We cannot believe that we have reached the last few days of the Jesus is Bae Challenge. This is crazy. It's day 29 out of 31!

This week there is no strong "concept," but we hope that you have tasted and seen that the Lord is good (Psalm 34:8). We hope that you have seen the benefits of spending time with God on a consistent basis, and we pray that you established some sort of routine that works best for you and your schedule. We hope that what began this month will continue for a lifetime.

Seriously, we pray that this challenge blessed you as much as it has blessed us! We are so incredibly humbled that God allowed us to embark with you on a journey of growing into greater intimacy with Him.

As we wrap things up, our message to you this week is simple: finish strong. Keep pressing into God and squeeze out every little bit that you can get from this challenge. And then continue to run this race with endurance.

There is SO much more to God, and He wants to reveal more of

Himself to you DAILY. He's alive, and He has plenty more to say. Not just for thirty-one days, but for the rest of your life.

We encourage you to continue the following:

- Prioritizing time with Jesus
- Growing in communication with Him
- Remaining open to Him and accountable and transparent with community on the topics of discontentment and habitual sin
- Regularly going on dates with Jesus

As you move forward, maybe you want to dedicate two weeks or a month for each topic we covered! Or you can do Hanha's favorite: read the Bible from the start of Genesis to the end of Revelation. Whatever you decide, don't stop seeking God! This is just the beginning.

DAY 29 - GALATIANS 6

In these last few days, we want to encourage you to be consistent in spending time with Jesus daily. Many of us know that consistency is important, but do we really know why? When you give up too quickly, you can miss your opportunity to see your goal come to fruition. When it comes to spending time with Jesus, you may lose your opportunity to learn more about God, learn more about you, and learn more about the purpose that He has for you.

> *"Let us not become weary in doing good, for at the proper time we will reap a harvest if we do not give up."*
>
> — *GALATIANS 6:9, NIV*

These thirty-one days have been a seed that you've planted, where you have invested in your relationship with God. There will be times when you may want to stop, but you cannot do this! The Bible does not say that it's possible, but that you WILL reap your harvest if you do not give up. So the question becomes what harvest you will miss out on because of your failure to keep going.

We were listening to this podcast, and we loved the way the preacher described the beauty of small beginnings. He said that we must learn to honor the small beginnings because if small weren't important, God would take us straight to big. This is such a huge life principle because if you think about anything you do in life or person you connect with, there is some form of consistency that has nurtured that goal or relationship.

The first time you get disappointed or feel unmotivated to read your Bible or talk to God isn't a sign that you should give up. In fact, it's a clear sign that you should keep going and many scriptures in the Bible talk about perseverance. Try these:

And I am sure of this, that He who began a good work in you will bring it to completion at the day of Jesus Christ.

— PHILIPPIANS 1:6, ESV

You need to persevere so that when you have done the will of God, you will receive what he has promised.

— HEBREWS 10:36, NIV

Let's discuss the areas in your life where you can apply this concept.

1. Prayer

This is SO important. As you've learned through this book, being consistent in your prayer life helps you to connect and build your relationship with God. It allows you to deepen your intimacy with Him so that you can intercede on behalf of other people and be a better witness to those who are in need of Christ's love. Don't give up!

2. Relationships

We still remember times when we have looked back at some of our relationships and often find ourselves close to tears because we wouldn't have been able to enjoy our friendships or relationships had we given up on them. Even Jesus was consistent with twelve people in His life. We're sure He would have rather dropped Peter on several occasions, but He continued to pursue them.

We must live in the same way. Find the people in your life with whom you want to nurture and cultivate a relationship. Is it the friend who annoys you sometimes but brings you joy? The friend who is so far from God and you have no idea if he or she will ever find Him? The mentor who keeps rescheduling the times you both are supposed to spend together? Don't give up!

3. Purpose

Whether that's starting a business, being the best mom to your child, or following your calling, you must remain consistent in it. The best part is that you can rely on Galatians 6:9. The Bible doesn't say that it's possible or that you can, it says that you WILL reap your harvest if you don't give up. Decide to keep going even when you are being impatient or don't feel like it.

Action Item/Reflection:

1. In what areas of your life do you need to be more consistent? Write it down here.

2. What action steps are you going to take so that you are more consistent?

DAY 30 - HEBREWS 12

1. Therefore, since we are surrounded by so great a cloud of witnesses, let us also lay aside every weight, and sin which clings so closely, and let us run with endurance the race that is set before us,
2. looking to Jesus, the founder and perfecter of our faith, who for the joy that was set before him endured the cross, despising the shame, and is seated at the right hand of the throne of God.

– Hebrews 12:1–2, ESV

According to commentary from the ESV Bible, the cloud of witnesses that this verse is referring to are the heroes of the faith. The ones who suffered and endured so that today you can read scripture, be encouraged, and find hope.

This life is a long-distance race that we are running. The finish line is heaven and eternity with God. At the finish line there will be no more pain, suffering, or sin. At the finish line, you will experience the victory that you have read about for a long time.

Sometimes during this race, you might have to take a breather. You might have to walk a few miles. You might face setbacks and completely stop running. You will encounter obstacles and hurdles that will trip you and cause you to fall and scrape your knees. You will pass through hills and run down valleys. Along the race, you may reach crossroads where you don't know what direction to turn.

This race is no easy one to run. It is the hardest you will ever face. But imagine Noah, Abraham, Moses, Isaiah, Paul, Mary, Joseph,

Ruth, Esther, the disciples, and all of the greats screaming your name on the sidelines and cheering you on.

Imagine God the Father, Jesus, and the Holy Spirit rooting for you. Picture Jesus praying for you (Romans 8:34; Hebrews 7:25), and imagine the Holy Spirit running with you nourishing you along the way.

Imagine the Father at that finish line waiting for you with open arms with a medal in hand and a mansion that He has prepared for you. Imagine Him giving you the biggest and warmest hug and congratulating you, saying, "My daughter, my son, well done my good and faithful servant. You ran the race well (Matthew 25:21)."

Friend, this is what you have to look forward to. Does that give you chills? Victory is yours! Continue to run the race and run it well. We love you and are cheering you on!

Action Items/Reflections:

1. What weights, sins, relationships, etc. are weighing you down in your race and hindering you from running your race well?

2. How are you feeling at this time in your race? Are you running up a hill, down a valley, have you stopped, tripped over an obstacle, or struggling to gather the strength to keep running? List where you are.

3. Now close your eyes and picture the cloud of witnesses cheering you on, Jesus praying for you, the Holy Spirit with you, God the Father awaiting you at the finish line.

4. What steps do you feel the Lord is asking you to take so that you can dust yourself off and continue to run your race well?

DAY 31 - LUKE 5

Jesus has just begun His ministry, and we catch Him as He's about to give a sermon. There are a lot of people gathering around, so Jesus gets innovative. He notices a boat on the edge of the shore and He knows if He can use it, people will not only be able to see Him, but His voice will also carry because the sound will reflect off the water.

The only problem is that the boat is not His, but Jesus is bold enough to ask the owner if He can borrow it. Fast forward a couple of verses and we learn that Jesus asks this same owner aka Simon Peter to follow Him. But before Jesus ever calls Peter to be His disciple, there are several observations we can learn.

1. Peter was working before He was called.
2. Peter was willing to be used in a small way first.
3. Peter was obedient.

It is important to notice the order of this because God is a God of order. We see so many examples of this throughout the Bible. David was tending sheep in the pasture (1 Samuel 16). Gideon was threshing wheat (Judges 6). Elisha was plowing fields (1 Kings 19). And Peter was washing nets.

All of them were working hard and focusing on the task assigned to them before ever being called or anointed for their purpose. In the same way, we must learn to be faithful to what we've been assigned. Sometimes, we want God to perform miracles in our lives when we have yet to be committed to the responsibilities He has given us stewardship over.

We're not saying God wants you to have a boring or hard life. In fact, we believe that He wants you to have the opposite! He has great plans for you, and His plans are better than anything you can think or imagine. But are you tending your sheep, threshing your wheat, or plowing your field? Are you working hard at the job you have even though you don't like it?

Or maybe God has asked to use you in a small way, but were you willing to say yes and serve Him? Are you willing to take out the trash even though your skill set matches that of an executive? Are you willing to serve your significant other even when they have wronged you? Are you willing to let Jesus use your boat just as Peter did? Willing to spend time in your Word and prayer even when it feels like you don't have time? Even when you haven't received what God has promised?

Because when we look back at the scripture, it was only then after Peter was working, after Peter was willing that Jesus performed a miracle in his life. AND THEN calls him to be one of the twelve disciples. But let's not miss that Peter's purpose was contingent on his obedience. We don't know if Jesus would have extended the invitation to Peter had he not been obedient, but we do know that Peter would have missed his blessing.

As we wrap up this devotional book, we ask that you pause, think, and reflect on your own life. We want nothing more than for you to grow into the person that God has called you to be and do the things that He has called you to do. We pray that you have grown over these past thirty-one days in a way that you can't explain. We pray that you have gained a new perspective on the love God has for you and how to live your life His way.

Your relationship with Christ will continue to grow even after you finish this book. But we hope you truly discovered what it means to be in a relationship with Him. Most of all, we pray that we have ignited a new passion inside you that will help you keep pursuing Him with your whole heart.

We leave you with some final encouragement. Continue to position your heart towards God. Take what we have taught and apply it to your life. Everything that you go through is for a specific purpose, and we know that God allowed you to read this book for a reason. You are so special to Him and these thirty-one days were just the beginning. We just can't wait to see what He does in your life next!

Action Item/Reflection:

1. Can you honestly say that you are working hard in the season that you are in? In what ways can you be more like Peter when it comes to serving God with a willing heart?

2. Do you struggle with being willing or obedient? Ask God to help you focus on Him and live a life that is pleasing to Him.

WEEK 5 REFLECTION

As we wrap up, write how you plan to take what you learned through this challenge and apply it to your daily life. How can you continue to be consistent in spending time with God and growing in your relationship with Him?

9 781595 559265